Enterprise Blockchain

A Definitive Handbook

By Navveen Balani & Rajeev Hathi

Enterprise Blockchain

A Definitive Handbook

By Navveen Balani & Rajeev Hathi

Introduction

Before we start with a formal introduction to blockchain, let us take you for a moment to a possible future that should realize sooner than we expect.

You are on a vacation outside your home country, at a shopping mall and receive a notification saying there is a sale on luxurious watches. You haven't been to this store before. You pick up a watch and you wonder if the watch is genuine and worth the price. You start a mobile application and place it on the watch. The application recognizes the watch and displays the complete lifecycle of the watch, like where it was manufactured and the GPS coordinates, what parts make up the watch, where it was designed, when it left the manufacturing unit, who was the dealer, custom clearance certificate, what is the warranty period, how much custom duty you need to pay (if any) if you bring this watch back to your home country and even showing and comparing similar watches. You purchase the watch based on these details and now feel even more connected to the watch brand and establish a trust with the shopping store for selling genuine products.

Take another example; you need to transfer money overseas, you open a mobile application, provide the beneficiary mobile number and money is transferred instantly. You can even select from the multiple transfer rates from multiple providers, view their ratings and choose one of them. You now have full control on how you can move your money across the globe without any central authority.

You are heading back to the airport and receive a message on your instant messenger; the message gets blocked instantly, the messenger classifies this as fake news. You are saved from distraction and later check why the message was blocked.

So far, we talked about consumer applications; let's take an example of a complex B2B process like an international trade finance which currently takes days to complete the trade process. If the entire workflow is automated, self-regulated and equipped with enough consensus between various parties carrying out the trade, it can provide a window of opportunity for new buyers and sellers to handshake, implement and execute trade seamlessly with lot of trust and confidence.

In all the scenarios that we described earlier and possibly in all our future applications, data would be a central point for businesses, consumers, and even system interaction. For businesses, data and its state would be used to establish trust and compliance between parties and for optimizing the businesses. For consumers, it would be providing a better experience, personalized engagements and even authenticity of data, be it for news, price or an event. For systems, data would be crucial to establish the trust and compliance for autonomous functionality between devices in a connected world.

Now in a data-driven world, you need to establish trust and compliance between parties, you need governance, regulation and accountability through automated workflow and digital contracts rather than central authority and finally a piece of technology that can enable to realize this goal. Once these basic parameters are enabled, it opens endless opportunities to move any value (from services to digital assets) across the network in a secure and transparent way. The technology enabler that can aid in realizing this opportunity is blockchain.

We view blockchain as an enabler to provide consensus of data. The consensus can be between business-to-business, business-to-consumer or consumer-to-consumer. We call blockchain an enabler, as blockchain alone will not lead to realizing the opportunities we talked about earlier. The combinatorial power of blockchain, smart contracts, and technologies like IoT & Artificial Intelligence would enable to deliver value-driven intelligent applications.

While we described our vision, we are probably at the first generation of blockchain implementation where technologies are still evolving, and use cases are being realized.

Through this book, we aim to provide a reference for building any blockchain application. The book comprises of 3 Chapters. In Chapter 1, we start with providing a neutral vision and architecture for blockchain, without getting into vendor implementations. In chapter 2 and 3, we will demonstrate the working of two widely used blockchain implementations – Ethereum and IBM Hyperledger Fabric respectively and build an end-to-end demo using a hands-on approach. The source code for the book is available on GitHub, and all demos can be carried out in a local environment.

To summarize, as part of the book, we would cover the following -

- A vendor-neutral architecture for building blockchain applications.
- A detailed introduction to Ethereum and its core components. We would set up a local instance of Ethereum and build end-to-end applications on Ethereum blockchain using a hands-on approach. At the end, we would cover topics around extension to Ethereum blockchain, integration with the external world and the future of smart contracts.
- A detailed introduction to IBM Hyperledger and its core components. We would cover the enterprise capabilities provided by IBM Hyperledger 1.0. At the end, we would set up a local instance of Hyperledger 1.0 and build end-to-end applications on Hyperledger blockchain using a hands-on approach.

Our goal in this book is to provide a simplistic view of blockchain technology. The concepts and references laid down in the book will help you to build any real-world blockchain application. Our aim is to keep the book short, relevant, provide practical guidance and enough information to our readers to be productive.

The blockchain book is part of our "The Definitive handbook" series. Our vision in the – "The Definitive handbook" series is to enable our readers to understand the technology in simple terms and provide a go-to reference and a recipe for building any real-world application using the latest technology.

This is our second – "Definitive handbook" series work, the first being – "Enterprise IoT" which got acknowledged as one of the Top Computing book for 2016 by computingreview.com (http://computingreviews.com/recommend/bestof/notableitems.cfm?bestYear=2016).

Stay tuned for the third series in the book, which is about "Real Artificial Intelligence", planned to be released next year. For details, kindly visit this link - http://navveenbalani.com/index.php/books/real-ai-book/

For any comments, suggestions or queries, please reach us at enterpriseblockchainbook@gmail.com or visit http://navveenbalani.com/index.php/articles/enterprise-blockchain-book/

Table of Contents

Chapter 1. Introduction to Blockchain

In this chapter, we will introduce blockchain and the core building blocks of a blockchain platform. Our intent is to provide a vendor neutral, generic reference architecture that can be used for building any blockchain applications.

Introduction to Blockchain

Blockchain can be termed as another hype or buzzword making its way to mainstream IT. It is a technology that will dramatically transform the way businesses are conducted. Today, organizations big or small operate in a network. It may have a customer, supplier, distributor, financial intermediaries, global and local partners and so on. They all collaborate and conduct economic activities to achieve certain common set of goals. It's a complex web of business entities that make money by offering services to each other. In business terms, exchange of goods and services (also known as assets) is called a transaction. It is a formal transfer of value and ownership of an asset from one entity to another, i.e., parties to the business. Transactions between these entities must be recorded and maintained in a book of account also called a ledger. Each business entity or organization maintains its own ledger, which consists of day-to-day transactions. Third party intermediary often does the bookkeeping or maintaining of the ledger. This obviously leads to increase in cost and in some way duplication of efforts as each entity in the business network maintains its own ledger of transactions. There is no clarity or transparency as to how the transactions are recorded and settled and the process of reconciliation is often time-consuming. In a nutshell, the current handling of accounts among the business network is less transparent and inefficient. So, what is the technology solution for this problem?

The solution lies in creating a technology infrastructure that can distribute or share the copy of ledger to all the entities in the business network. This is where the blockchain comes into the picture. Blockchain is a distributed ledger protocol that offers a more unique and innovative approach towards maintaining transactions among business entities. Transactions are validated by all the entities and created as unit of blocks. Blockchain architecture can be applied to public or private business network. With public applications, every business entity can view and validate the transactions, though no one can alter it. In a private setup, ledger is permissioned, which means only authorized entities can act (like validate or view) on transactions. Transactions, in general, cannot be tampered with, i.e., its state cannot be altered. It means blockchain ledgers are immutable. Transaction payloads are secured using cryptographic hash and digitally signed using public/private key thereby certifying provenance. The digital signature proves the identity or the ownership of the transaction or the digital token (asset) that is being transacted. The blockchain transactions are generated with network-wide consensus without the need of central server or authority. The consensus here means all the entities in a business network agree on the validity, state of data and originality of the transaction.

Note – Understanding blockchain 1.0 and 2.0.
Bitcoin-based blockchain is popularly termed as blockchain 1.0. It is modeled around simple database concepts with data insertion (transaction recording) happening sequentially in the distributed ledger. There was no special logic involved. Then came the modern blockchain applications that introduced the concept of smart contracts. The smart contracts came under the blockchain 2.0 umbrella. Smart contract represents a software code that performs some logic, then just recording transactions. Blockchain platforms like IBM

HyperLedger, Microsoft Bletchley, Ethereum, etc. are all part of blockchain 2.0 world.

Here are the benefits of a blockchain network in a nutshell:

- The blockchain network manages the transactions without the need of any intermediary or central authority. It is self-regulated and automated using smart contracts and consensus protocol.
- All the business entities are equipped with their copy of ledgers, and therefore, the information is shared and transparent across the network
- With blockchain, the data or the transaction record is up to date, verified and consistent as all the business entities are involved in performing the validation.
- Reliable and highly available as there is no central point of failure.
- There is a significant reduction in cost as a business need not maintain its own ledger and managed by any third-party intermediaries.
- Transaction settlement and the process of reconciliation are automatic and almost immediate. Unlike the manual process, it does not require any mandatory number of business working days to make the settlement.
- It mandates the use of single ledger where all the transactions of a defined business network are recorded. It, therefore, removes the data redundancy and the need to maintain separate ledger by each business entity.

A blockchain network is setup based on the following principles:

Consensus: The network must be in the state of consensus, i.e., the validity of the blocks of transactions must be validated and agreed or accepted by all the nodes (or designated nodes) in the blockchain network.

Provenance: Provenance generally means place of origin. In the context of blockchain, it refers to the origin of the digital tokens or assets. The nodes in the network must know who is the owner of the digital asset and also track the change of ownership.

Immutability: In a blockchain network, the ledger cannot be tampered with once the transactions are recorded. A ledger may have valid or invalid transactions. An invalid transaction is addressed by adding a new valid transaction of the same value. Data in the blockchain network is append-only and not subject to modification.

Components of Blockchain

The following components are the principal building blocks that can be perceived as the architectural cornerstones of an enterprise blockchain:

Digital Tokens

Anything that can be transacted over the blockchain takes the form of digital tokens. Digital tokens represent assets that hold value and have some form of ownership. Assets can be a physical asset like a car, house, cash, etc. and non-physical or tangible assets like patents, copyrights, intellectual property, etc. Digital tokens are secured using cryptographic hash algorithms which takes care of confidentiality aspect. Tokens also have one more level of security in terms of authentication and authorization. It must be signed by the owner to maintain secured identity. The concept of

authentication and authorization can be achieved with Public Key
Infrastructure (PKI) using private/public key cryptography.

Smart Contract

Smart Contract is one of the core component of modern day blockchain or
the so called blockchain 2.0. It's a contract which defines and executes
transactions in the form of a software code written in a programming
language of choice. It comprises of business operations that act on the state
of the blockchain ledger. It contains business logic conditions that affect the
state of a digital token (asset) in terms of its value and ownership. The
conditional logic or the business rules compiled together makes up a well-
defined contract that suggests how this transaction will be carried out and
hence, the term 'smart' contract. The smart contract can be written in any
programming language like Java, NodeJS, Scala etc. Smart contract can be
made secured through encryption and digital signing.

Ledger

The blockchain ledger is an electronic health record of a business. It is a
system of records containing all transactions in the order of its occurrence
in a given business network. These transactions are initiated by the client
application and executed using smart contracts. The transactions by itself
represent some kind of transfer of value of digital tokens recorded in the
ledger. The ledger must be immutable, i.e., no one should be able to tamper
with the transactions, once recorded in the ledger. The blockchain ledger is
shared across all entities in a business network. Each node in the network
maintains its own copy of the ledger. In a private blockchain network,
ledgers are often permissioned, which means only authorized entities can
act on a ledger.

Security

Security in the blockchain can be enforced using authentication and authorization. Different form of policies can be created that can communicate different level of access controls for every step in the blockchain workflow. One possible example could be say, only nodes with appropriate permission levels can perform ledger validation. Another aspect of security in the blockchain is the trust based communication. Trust based communication can be established using cryptography digital certificates. Every transaction occurring between entities in the network can be digitally signed to protect its identity and verified using private/public key pair. The transaction payload itself can be encrypted using crypto hash algorithms to maintain confidentiality. In a public blockchain, every node in the network has the visibility and access to the transaction and block creation. In a permissioned blockchain, ledger access and manipulation to the ledger is controlled through the use of access control policies and creation of private conduits with only nodes within that conduit can transact with each other.

Consensus

Consensus means agreement in majority. In a blockchain, all the nodes are equipped with their copy of the ledger that is synchronized as and when the new transaction occurs. Every new transaction when validated and accepted by all the nodes in the network, the ledger is said to be in the state of consensus. It means all the participants in the network agree to and accept the current state of ledger. There are many aspects of the blockchain workflow where the consensus is required. Consensus by itself can be adhering to different policies and thereupon validating the same. The nodes refer to existing set of checklist or rules or policies to validate different lifecycle phase of transactions, right from its inception until it is finally recorded in the blockchain. The consensus in some way implies network integrity. The consensus as such cannot be broken through any kind of corrupt or hacking practice. In order to break the consensus, a whole new blockchain will need to be created with 'broken records, ' and that can be a huge task. There are different industry-wide consensus protocols one can use in the blockchain application viz. Proof-Of-Work, Proof-of-Stake, Practical Byzantine Fault Tolerance and many more. We will briefly discuss the popular algorithms in the 'Consensus Algorithm' section.

Nodes

Nodes are the most important component in the network deployment model of blockchain. A node can be a physical box or different logical processes (nodes) in one physical box. They are the backbone of the blockchain architecture. Nodes collaborate with each other to form a peer model and work together to arrive at the consensus and keep the network in a consistent state. They typically validate and execute transactions in the network. Nodes in a blockchain can play various roles like the miners, validators, orderer, monitoring node, health check node, etc. (For more on miners and mining concept, you can refer to chapter 2 that explains permissionless Ethereum blockchain.) These roles assume more significance in a permissioned enterprise blockchain scenario. This is because in a permissioned blockchain, the network is managed and controlled using access control policies and these policies can be attached to the role of each node in the network. Each node in the network, by fulfilling its role equipped with set of policies, forms a group of powerful trusted entities that keeps the entire blockchain network more secure, stable, resilient and consistent.

Reference Architecture

Blockchain design of today has moved beyond cryptocurrency. It has evolved into a platform that supports industry-wide use cases suitable for public and enterprise needs. The reference architecture shown below will serve as a foundation for building or implementing blockchain applications for industry-wide use cases. It depicts a layered architecture that provides components and services necessary to implement blockchain applications for enterprise needs. It can be used to develop a blockchain of single or multiple networks (involving multiple business units or organizations) based on the business goals and objectives. One can follow the reference architecture to design both permissioned (private) as well as permissionless (public) blockchain applications.

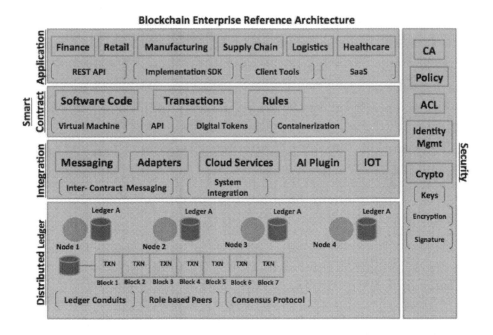

Blockchain Enterprise Reference Architecture

The above reference architecture can be used to build any blockchain applications. The architecture is divided into logical layers of importance. These layers are Application, Smart Contract, Integration, Distributed Ledger and Security. Let's look at each of these layers and its components:

Application

The application layer is where your end user or client application sits. The client application typically kick starts your business workflow by initiating a transaction. The transactions are executed by the nodes using smart contract. The client application could be implemented in any software language and can run on a wide variety of operating systems. The application could use a command line interface (CLI) tool as provided by any blockchain framework implementation or it could use language specific SDK (Software Development Kit) to communicate with nodes on the network. As the blockchain evolves beyond its traditional image of digital crypto currency based network, we are seeing different types of clients and tools supporting the blockchain framework. The client application can also listen to various types of events occurring on the blockchain network and perform the necessary actions on those events. The event may be as simple as providing status update to the application from the network. One can also have a separate dedicated application to monitor the blockchain network.

Smart Contract

Smart contract is a software code that represents transactions in the blockchain network. It is a collection of business rules or conditions that are invoked by the nodes in the blockchain network. Smart contract can have its own execution runtime or a virtual machine environment. It can be made to run in a secured context, like a virtualized container. Smart contract can be implemented in any software languages, the popular being, but not limited to, Java, Python, Go, JavaScript and Scala. Smart contract can be also written as services and placed in registries so that client can look up for the same in a location independent way. The registries can be secured, and access can be controlled so that only authorized clients can act upon that contract. Smart contract itself can be made secured using cryptographic hash algorithms so that it's content (software code and related metadata) are made confidential. Smart contract can also be programmed to communicate or broadcast transaction state transitions in the form of events. It could be lifecycle events of the contract itself. The application client can listen to these events and handle them accordingly.

Integration

In today's world of disruptive technologies where application integration and communication has become so imperative, no one platform can stand in isolation. Blockchain is no different. Blockchain network should be able to access any data outside of the network. The data could be part of any external application or system that can provide significant value to the blockchain workflow. Similarly, external system must also be able to communicate with the blockchain network. One approach could be to setup an external event hub, as a medium to exchange data with external systems through event processing. An external application can listen on to a specific event on the hub and accordingly perform some task. On the other hand, a smart contract can listen to events coming from external systems and accordingly execute the business function. The following section explains some other interesting use cases in the integration scenario:

Artificial Intelligence (AI) Integration

Blockchain as we know is essentially a distributed ledger with a decentralized and automated approach towards transaction settlement process based on consensus. So, where does AI fits into blockchain? AI can be influenced by data. Blockchain is a database with loads of transactions that can be made available to branches of AI like machine learning that can apply complex algorithms on data to optimize a particular business function. The branch of AI can also be used to improve the overall business process or workflow. AI algorithms can detect significant anomalies and perform predictive modeling or analysis to find indicators that can reduce the transaction cost and increase the revenue of business for all parties across the blockchain network. AI solutions can also be employed for consensus between systems that need to work autonomously. The combinatorial power of AI and blockchain could be a real game-changer in the future.

Cloud Integration

Blockchain architecture can be extended to implement a component hosted on the cloud that can provide application integration services like routing, data transformation, protocol translation, extended certificate authority etc. This component can act as a middleware, offering its capabilities as a 'blockchain as a service' function in the cloud. The blockchain implementation can provide adapters to connect to the middleware component from within the blockchain network and outside of the network. The blockchain middleware component can be hosted in a secured 'sandboxed' environment or inside a secured virtualized container. An external application can interact with the blockchain middleware using adapters and upon obtaining valid certificates to access the blockchain network.

IoT integration

A new wave of integration will involve arbitrary devices to communicate with the blockchain network. Different types of IoT devices or sensors can inject data into the blockchain network that can then be validated by the blockchain nodes. A standardized middleware can be implemented that can take the data from the device and perform the necessary conversion and transformation of data as required by the blockchain network. The peers or the nodes in the blockchain network can then go about validating this data using a specific consensus algorithm using smart contracts.

Note - For more details on blockchain & IoT integration, refer to this overview article - http://navveenbalani.com/index.php/articles/blockchain-and-enterprise-iot/

Distributed Ledger

This distributed ledger is the core persistent layer in the blockchain architecture. It provides a decentralized and distributed database containing the transaction entries. These entries are recorded in the order of its occurrence and composed into hashed blocks. The database or the ledger, therefore, represents a chain of hashed blocks of transactions with each block referring to the previous block in the chain. The ledger is shared across the blockchain network, which means every node has a copy of the ledger, and each node verifies the transactions independently. When every node agrees and confirms the authenticity of the transaction, the ledger is said to be in consensus. The blockchain network uses different consensus algorithms to arrive at the consensus. The consensus algorithm is a set of rules and conditions that governs the transaction. The blockchain network implemented for the public has a permissionless ledger, while in a private network or a consortium, a ledger can be made permissioned. A permissioned ledger introduces some form of access control in the way transactions are accessed and managed.

Ledger Conduits

For a permissioned-based blockchain network, one can implement a pattern called ledger conduits. Conduits can be thought of as private channels in the blockchain network where two or more nodes perform transactions even more privately. The nodes must be members and authorized to use these conduits. Conduits are small networks inside a large network. Such a pattern further enforces security when implementing blockchain in an enterprise.

Consensus Algorithms

The blockchain network typically is governed by anonymous entities or nodes that are not trusted. The consensus is all about providing the trust factor in the network. Each node can update the blockchain network with data in the form of transaction that eventually needs to be verified before it can be offlcially recorded as part of block in the ledger. There are different consensus algorithms that convey how the block (of transactions) is created and validated, thereby enforcing trust in the network.

Practical Byzantine Fault Tolerance (PBFT)
This is the consensus based on majority. Each node updates and validates the blockchain network based on certain given set of rules or conditions. If majority of the nodes in the network reflects the same result upon update, then the network is said to be in consensus. There could be few rogue nodes that could violate the network rules, but their outcome is not

accepted as it goes against the accepted algorithm. The algorithm should fulfill the necessary conditions, and all the nodes must agree and execute the same conditions to derive at the desired output.

Proof-of-work (PoW)

One of the first and traditional algorithms devised is the Proof-of-Work. Bitcoin-based blockchain network and Ethereum use this algorithm. Unlike PBFT, PoW does not need consensus based on majority. It is an algorithm that takes enormous computing effort. Only nodes with greater computing power can take up the PoW. The first node that completes the task with the desired output gets a chance to create the block and is compensated for its efforts. PoW typically involves some kind of cryptographic hashing to achieve the desired target or outcome. We will talk of PoW in detail in Chapter 2.

Proof-of-Stake (PoS)

With PoW, one needs enormous computing power that results in high-energy consumption. This may not be desirable. PoS overcome this by providing an alternative approach called the stake of the user. The user possessing or owning highest digital currencies (or some asset) gets a chance to create the block in the blockchain network. So instead of investing in high power computing nodes, one can rather buy out cryptocurrency (or own assets) and increase their stake to validate and create a block of transactions.

Security

We talked about security earlier in the components of blockchain section. Security is one of the important components in the blockchain architecture. Based on the implementation of blockchain - whether permissionless or permissioned, required security and consensus strategies are applied. In public blockchain, every node can participate in the network, while in the permissioned network you have some form of access control that only allows required nodes to participate in a transaction.

Every entity in the blockchain network must be bound to an identity. In a permissionless network, entities are typically restricted to users participating in the transaction, while in case of a permissioned network, the entities comprise of organization, nodes, users and anything that has a role to play in the blockchain network.

For a permissioned blockchain, Public Key Infrastructure (PKI) platform can be used where a trusted Certificate Authority (CA) can issue crypto credentials. The crypto credentials could take the form of certificates and keys. Private keys can be used for signing and public key for verification. It results in a trusted network where all the participants know who they are and their roots of trust. Now as the parties involved in the blockchain network might leverage their own crypto credentials, possibly setting up their own CA, it is essential that the blockchain implementation provides a plug-and-play service or a level of abstraction to effectively manage, verify and validate entities using different security mechanism across the network.

In short, the blockchain security should be equipped with five effective measures viz. authentication, access control, integrity, confidentiality, and non-repudiation.

Summary

Blockchain can be thought of as a next wave of network revolution after the Internet, specifically in the business world. The self-regulated environment that offers consensus, provenances in terms of identity management, security in terms of cryptography and policies will pave the way for a new generation of applications that will provide a more robust infrastructure support to the blockchain network. There are many different flavors of blockchain existing today, from a permissionless ledger like Ethereum to a permissioned one like IBM HyperLedger. The industry use cases of blockchain have evolved from cryptography currency-centric financial domain to various other industries like Insurance, Supply Chain, Healthcare, IoT, etc. Based on the use cases, you would go with permissionless or permissioned blockchain or even a combination of two where public consensus would drive private business transactions.

Thinking in blockchain has already started, and the combinatorial power of Cloud, Big Data, AI, IoT and the Distributed Ledger will lead to innovative business solutions.

Chapter 2. Building Blockchain applications using Ethereum

In this chapter, we will introduce a permissionless blockchain implementation called Ethereum. The chapter will cover the core features of Ethereum platform, how to setup a local instance of Ethereum, deploy smart contracts and build an end-to-end sample application.

Introduction to Ethereum

As per the Ethereum website -

"Ethereum is a decentralized platform that runs smart contracts, applications that run exactly as programmed without the possibility of downtime, censorship, fraud or third party interference."

Let's understand this definition in a detail by understanding the terminology and core features of an Ethereum platform.

Core Features of Ethereum platform

In this section, we will talk about the core features of the Ethereum platform.

Application

An application in an Ethereum platform is referred to as a DApp (decentralized application). The DApp typically comprises of a frontend and a backend code. The frontend code is developed using programming languages like JavaScript. The frontend code communicates with the backend code on the blockchain network. The backend code is referred to as a smart contract and is typically developed using a higher-level language like Solidity. The smart contract runs on the decentralized Ethereum network. The DApp maps to the application layer of our reference architecture.

Note - The frontend part of the DApp does not run on Ethereum network. So in an Ethereum context, a DApp could be simply referred to as the smart contract running in the Ethereum network.

Smart Contract

We had described smart contract earlier in Chapter 1. Smart Contract defines and executes transactions in the form of a software code. It comprises of operations that act on the state of the blockchain.

This smart contract acts as a digital contract, which can be used to move value and ownership of assets between parties in a given network or across networks. These contracts can be between a consumer to consumer - like a wire transfer between individuals using their cell phones without any intermediary, a business to business - like a trade finance contract where multiple parties are involved viz. exporter bank, importer bank and shipment vendor, a business to consumer - like an insurance or a health contract which rewards people for their good health behaviors or even between system to system - which enables system to work in a secure and autonomous way, for instance, a contract that defines whether a new device can connect seamlessly to your connected home.

The smart contract in an Ethereum network runs inside an Ethereum Virtual Machine (EVM) and its available on every node in the Ethereum network. Every node has the same copy of the smart contract and runs the same code/logic. We would go through the process of developing and deploying a smart contract during the course of this chapter.

The Smart contract maps to the smart contract layer of our reference architecture.

Note – Solidity is compiled into bytecode that is executed on EVM.

Ether and Gas

To run applications on the public Ethereum blockchain network, you need ethers. Ether is a form of payment – a digital fuel that client applications need to pay in order to deploy the smart contract and execute its operations. Each operation requires some computation; this computation work is referred to as a gas. Different operations require different gas units, which is auto calculated by the system. Based on the gas required, the client needs to pay the appropriate ethers. Think of ether being paid for a gas, as a software service fee for executing the code on the network.

Note - Ether is a form of digital currency, similar to Bitcoin. But instead of using ether as a market currency, the design of Ethereum platform uses ether as a means to run the decentralized applications.

Ethereum Wallet

The Ethereum Wallet allows you to hold and secure ethers and other crypto-assets created on Ethereum. It also allows you to write, deploy and use smart contracts. We would soon see Ethereum Wallet in action as part of our sample application demonstration. The Ethereum Wallet can be mapped to the application layer of our reference architecture, which provides a capability to interact with our Ethereum network.

One important point is to understand how consensus is reached across the Ethereum network and data (i.e., blocks) committed to Ethereum. In the next section, we will talk about this in detail.

Consensus Algorithm in Ethereum

We briefly discussed in chapter 1, different consensus algorithms like Proof-of-Work (PoW), Proof-of-Stake (PoS) and Practical Byzantine Fault Tolerance (PBFT). Ethereum currently uses the PoW algorithm and the plan is to move to PoS in a later release. Let's understand the PoW consensus algorithm in more detail and what problem it is trying to solve in a decentralized public network.

Ethereum blockchain uses permissionless consensus. Permissionless here means that any node can join and participate in the network and execute or validate the transactions. Out of all the public nodes in the network, majority of the nodes, say 51% out of 100 must agree on the validity of the transaction to arrive at a consensus. Once consensus is reached, the transaction is committed to Ethereum. Now, in the absence of a central governing authority, how can one assure that 51% of these nodes are genuine and no one has added or manipulated nodes to drive transaction in their favor. That's where the PoW algorithm is applied to drive consensus throughout the network.

The following points explains the PoW algorithm in simple terms

- In a PoW based Ethereum network, each node needs to solve a mathematical puzzle to propose their transaction or to be more precise, an intent to create and commit the block. To solve this mathematical puzzle, it requires lot of computation, power (energy) and time in terms of CPU resources. The nodes solving this puzzle are referred to as miners.

- The mathematical puzzle is all about finding a message digest based on input message + the digest of the previous block.

---

*Note – A message **digest** is a cryptographic **hash** function containing a set of digits created by a one-way **hashing** formula.*
Digest basically ensures data is not altered and the integrity of the message is maintained between the sender and receiver.

- The mathematical puzzle should be less than the difficulty level of the system. The difficulty level is an arithmetically derived number set by the system. For more details, refer to the example below.

- Once the puzzle is solved, all other nodes should agree to the solution and apply the same formula to arrive at a consensus.

- The node that is the first to solve the mathematical puzzle, and eventually verified and agreed by all other nodes is rewarded for its work. In the Ethereum network, this would imply a node being rewarded with some ethers for solving the puzzle.

Given below is an example of PoW algorithm.

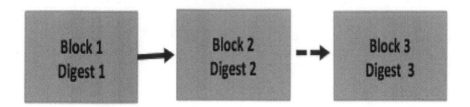

Let's assume there is a chain of 2 blocks already committed on the network. A new block 3 needs to be added to the existing chain. Let's understand the sequence of flow as to how this third block of transaction would be committed:

Every node in the network will take up the challenge of creating the third block and committing the same to the blockchain. For this to achieve, each of the nodes will try to solve a mathematical equation. In the context of Ethereum, it is a digest value that needs to be created and it has to be less than some difficulty level preset by the system. The mathematical equation could be something like the following:

Problem to solve: Calculate digest (3) which should be < (less than) the difficulty level

The equation and its context:

Let's assume the difficulty level is preset as 000000000000000..... 781. Now the *digest (3)* is calculated using hash algorithm (say *sha256*) and by creating the hash of the values: block 2, digest 2 and nonce

Note: Nonce can be any arbitrary value that is incremented every time the node makes an attempt to find the correct *digest(3)* value. In short, nonce is incremented to find a solution to the equation.

Overview of the solution:

Now, each node would start solving this equation by incrementing the nonce value. Let's say B3 is the new block to be committed, B2 is the previous block i.e. block 2 and D is the difficulty level. If equation is solved the result is Yes, else it is No. The following snippet shows how a node tries to solve the equation:

- Iteration 1 - Sha256 (Block 3, Block 2, 1) < D Outcome – No

- Iteration 2 - Sha256 (Block 3, Block 2, 2) < D Outcome – No

...

- Iteration 2000008 - Sha256 (Block 3, Block 2, 4000008) < D Outcome – Yes

The miner node will keep trying until the outcome is Yes. It is like a rat race where every node attempts to be the first to get the outcome as 'Yes'. As you can see from the above snippet, at nonce value 4000008, the equation is solved, i.e., the *digest(3)* value is less than the difficulty level. The node that solves this equation propagates the nonce value of 4000008 to all the other nodes in the network for verification. All other nodes would simply take this nonce value and verify if it is indeed less than the difficulty level. The other nodes just need one-step to verify this equation with least computing power.

Once verified, the block will get committed, i.e., chained to the previous block and the miner is rewarded with ethers for the work done.

Note – As you can see in above example, the blockchain is a chain of hashes, each linked to previous one, i.e., Digest of 3 contains Digest 2, Digest of 2 contains Digest 1 and so on. Adding a new block in between by an intruder implies changing the entire hash sequence till the very beginning, which seems virtually impossible.

Use case

In this section, we will build a crowdsourcing application using an Ethereum platform. Our crowdsourcing application has the following requirements;

- Register a project that needs funding. The minimum funding amount for a project can't be changed after the initial setup.
- Multiple funders should be able to fund the project.
- View the status of the funding at any interval.
- Update the status of project as it goes through the process of funding.
- Funding of the project can be closed explicitly. If the funding is closed explicitly, the funders should get their respective amount automatically.

We will create a smart contract that will implement the above use case requirement. To realize our use case, we will create a local private instance of Ethereum, where all functions of the use case will be executed locally.

Setting Ethereum on Local Environment

To set up an Ethereum network on a local environment, you will need to download one of its implementation. We would go with Go Ethereum.

Go Ethereum is an implementation of Ethereum in Go programming language. To get started, download Go Ethereum a.k.a. Geth for your operating system from https://geth.ethereum.org/downloads/. The current version of Geth at the time of writing this book is 1.7.1.

Tip – If you are on a MAC, use the following details to quickly install Ethereum using brew.

$ brew tap ethereum/ethereum

$ brew install ethereum

To bootstrap your private Ethereum network, we need to create a starting block or the first block termed as genesis block. A genesis block is the block that contains configuration details of the Ethereum network. The following JSON file is a sample custom genesis configuration that you will use to bootstrap the Ethereum private network.

```
{
  "config": {
      "chainId": 1,
      "homesteadBlock": 0,
      "eip155Block": 0,
      "eip158Block": 0
   },
  "alloc"     : {},
  "coinbase"  : "0x0000000000000000000000000000000000000000",
  "difficulty" : "0x20000",
  "extraData"  : "",
  "gasLimit"  : "0x2fefd8",
  "nonce"     : "0x0000000000000050",
  "mixhash"   :
"0x0000000000000000000000000000000000000000000000000000000000000000",
```

```
  "parentHash" :
"0x000000000000000000000000000000000000000000000000000000000000
00000",
  "timestamp" : "0x00"
}
```

The above configuration file named start.json specifies the fields in JSON format that sets up the Ethereum network. Some of the significant fields are *difficulty level, gas limit, nonce, mixhash* hash values (used for applying PoW), starting block number (i.e., *chainId*) and so on. You can also bootstrap the network with predefined wallet accounts and ether by specifying it in the *alloc* field. We will leave the *alloc* field blank for now, as we will focus on creating accounts and mining ethers locally as part of our application.

In the next section we will create the above genesis block and set up a local Ethereum network. To get started, download the project from the GitHub repository – https://github.com/enterprise-blockchain-book/first-edition.git.

Note - For more details on genesis block, refer to https://github.com/ethereum/go-ethereum/wiki/Private-network

---

Creating Genesis Block

As a first step, we will bootstrap a local Ethereum network by creating the genesis block using the above described start.json file. You can follow the below steps:

- Open a terminal or command prompt and navigate to ethereum/setup folder from the downloaded git project. Run the following command:

```
geth --datadir=./data init start.json
```

It will create the genesis block in the data folder. You should see a message at the end –"Successfully wrote genesis state"

- Next execute the following command to start a local instance of Ethereum using the data folder created in earlier step.

```
geth --networkid 999 --ipcpath ~/Library/Ethereum/geth.ipc --rpc --rpcaddr "127.0.0.1" --rpcapi="db,eth,net,web3,personal,web3" --rpcport "8545" --datadir=./data --rpccorsdomain "*" console
```

Note - For windows, use the same command without the ipcpath. -

```
geth --networkid 999 --rpc --rpcaddr "127.0.0.1" --rpcapi="db,eth,net,web3,personal,web3" --rpcport "8545" --datadir=./data --rpccorsdomain "*" console
```

The following provides the details of the above command line options:

- o networkid – The networkid value of 999 signifies a local environment. There are standard predefined networkid values from 1 to 5, like 1 for Frontier which connects to an actual Etherum network, 3 is for Ropsten which is a Test Ethereum network. Any value other than these predefined values implies a local instance.
- o ipcpath – This is the IPC endpoint file. IPC or interprocess communication allows local processes to communicate with geth using the IPC endpoint.
- o rpc - Enable remote procedure call of Geth APIs over HTTP JSON-RPC protocol.
- o rpcaddr and rpcport - Specify RPC address and RPC port
- o rpcapi – List of Geth APIs that would be enabled over RPC port

- ○ *datadir* – The data directory for the databases.
- ○ *rpccorsdomain* - Comma-separated list of domains from which to accept cross-origin requests from the browser. A value of "*" implies accept a request from all domains. Our web application will use XMLHttpRequest to interact with Ethereum node using RPC protocol.
- ○ *console* – This would start the geth node instance and open the console.

Note - To view all command line options, kindly visit https://github.com/ethereum/go-ethereum/wiki/Command-Line-Options.

After you execute the command, you would see the below set of messages being printed on the console, denoting IPC endpoint and RPC-HTTP location of the Ethereum node, along with the Geth JavaScript console welcome message. Let's refer to the said console as 'geth console', and we would reference this later in this chapter. You can also see some modules loaded at the end. We will use one of the module web3 API to invoke certain useful functions.

```
"INFO [08-15|17:55:27] IPC endpoint opened:
/Users/Navveen/Library/Ethereum/geth.ipc
INFO [08-15|17:55:27] HTTP endpoint opened:
http://127.0.0.1:8545
Welcome to the Geth JavaScript console!
instance: Geth/v1.6.1-stable-021c3c28/darwin-
amd64/go1.8.3 modules: admin:1.0 debug:1.0 eth:1.0
miner:1.0 net:1.0 personal:1.0 rpc:1.0 txpool:1.0 web3:1.0"
```

Creating Main Account

In this section, we would create our first account using geth console. Follow the steps below:

- On the geth console prompt, let's create an account by invoking the web3 API *personal.newAccount()* method. You can replace 'password' by the password of your choice..

```
> web3.personal.newAccount("password")
```

You will see the following public address and keystore location of the account. The first account is designated as the main account (a.k.a. etherbase) by default. This is the default address where the mining reward (i.e., ether) would be credited.

```
"0x42d187a0fce3392e853770d360e850f2ea1681bc"
> INFO [08-15|18:00:47] New wallet appeared
url=keystore:///Users/Navveen/Downlo... status=Locked
```

- You can view the list of accounts, by using the web3 API method *personal.listAccounts()* as shown below

```
> web3.personal.listAccounts
```

The above method will display the public address of the main account.

```
["0x42d187a0fce3392e853770d360e850f2ea1681bc"]
```

- Next, you would get the balance associated with the main account as

```
> web3.fromWei(eth.getBalance(eth.coinbase));
0
```

The *getBalance()* method returns 0, which is as expected as we do yet have any ethers in the account.

Creating Miners

In this section, we would start mining locally to add ethers to the main account. Follow the steps below:

- Open a new terminal or command prompt and type in the following command to connect to existing Ethereum geth node instance over IPC port that we had set up earlier. We will provide the path to the existing IPC endpoint location to the 'geth attach' command. Upon running the command it will open up the console. Let's refer to this console as 'geth sub-console'; we would reference this later in the chapter.

```
geth attach ~/Library/Ethereum/geth.ipc
```

Note - For windows, use the same command without specifying the ipc path as shown below. If you recall earlier while starting the geth instance we did not specify ipc path for windows.

```
geth attach
```

You should see the following message –

```
instance: Geth/v1.6.1-stable-021c3c28/darwin-amd64/go1.8.3
coinbase: 0x42d187a0fce3392e853770d360e850f2ea1681bc
at block: 0 (Thu, 01 Jan 1970 05:30:00 IST)
datadir: /Users/Navveen/Downloads/ethereum/setup/data
modules: admin:1.0 debug:1.0 eth:1.0 miner:1.0    net:1.0
personal:1.0 rpc:1.0 txpool:1.0 web3:1.0
```

- On the prompt, enter the following command

```
> miner.start(2)
```

This will start mining on the geth console. On the geth console, you should see the messages "committed new block" being printed. The value of 2 signifies the number of threads. It means the command will spawn two threads to perform mining in parallel. You can specify any number of threads. Please note that threads are expensive resources and therefore specifying large number of threads will take up more system memory.

You can stop the mining after 30 minutes, and you should have enough ethers in the main account. To stop mining, execute the following command

```
> miner.stop()
```

- Go back to the geth console and type in the following to get the balance of the main account.

```
> web3.fromWei(eth.getBalance(eth.coinbase));
```

You would see ethers in your account. For the crowdfunding application, we would need around 2000 ethers. So, make sure you have enough ethers; else you can start the mining process again by issuing commands in geth sub-console as described earlier.

With the main account setup with enough ether balance, next we will create additional accounts using the Ethereum Wallet application. We will also deploy and execute our smart contract using the said application.

Installing Ethereum Wallet

Ethereum Wallet provides a graphical interface to create and manage accounts and execute smart contracts. You can download the Ethereum Wallet for your operating system from the Download section at https://github.com/ethereum/mist/releases

Next, open the Ethereum Wallet, and this should connect to your running local Ethereum instance. You should see a message – *Private NET* on the application window as shown below. It effectively means the wallet is connected to the running local instance. Click on *Launch Application*.

You should see an *Account Overview* screen as shown in the figure below. The Accounts section contains the *Main Account* (*etherbase*) that we created earlier, along with the ether balance that was mined locally.

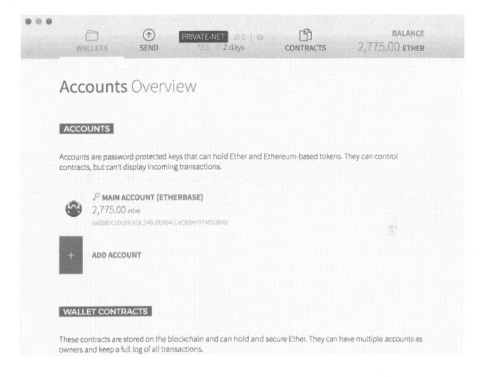

Creating Accounts

Next, we would create sample accounts for our crowdsourcing application. We will create total of three accounts, two funder accounts and one beneficiary account for which the money is being raised.

Earlier we created the main account using the Web3 APIs; this option provides an alternate way to create accounts using the wallet interface.

For creating accounts, click on the *Add Account* link. Enter the password for the account and confirm it. Next screen would display the password key files for your account and its path. If you plan to use your account on other machines or phones, you can simply import this key files to get access to your account.

Note – A pair of keys, a private key, and a public address defines every account in Ethereum. If you lose the key file, you will lose access to your account. So make sure to backup this key file when running in a production environment. The key file is available in Ethereum node's data directory. For Mac, this is located at ~/Library/Ethereum, for Linux - ~/.ethereum and for windows at C:\Users\%username%\%appdata%\Roaming\Ethereum.

The key file is a hidden file; so make sure you have enabled the appropriate option to view the hidden files.

Click on the newly created account. On the account details page, click on *Account 2* and rename it as *Funder1*. The following figure shows the details of *Funder1* account.

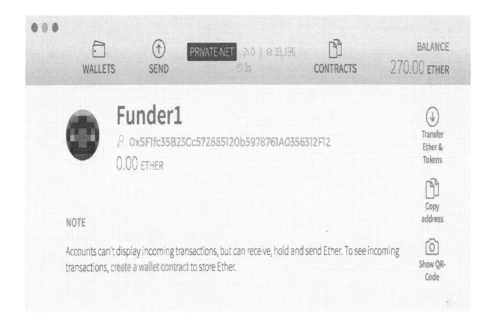

Now, click on the *copy address* link located on the right side. A warning window will be displayed as the account is on private network, click *copy anyway*.

Next, click on *Transfer Ether and Tokens*. On the *Send* tab, select *From* as the Main Account (Etherbase), and the *To* field should be populated with the address of the *Funder1* account. If not, paste the address that you copied in the earlier step. Enter amount as 1000. If you click on *Show More Options,* you can specify the fee you are willing to pay for executing this transaction in the blockchain network. You can also select a higher fee for faster processing of the transaction. Since this is a private network, drag the fee slider to Faster. The following figure shows the *Send* tab with these details. Click *Send.*

On the *Send transaction* window, specify the account password to confirm the transaction. In this page, you would see the gas price, the estimated consumption fee in ethers from earlier selected option and the maximum fee, which you are willing to pay for the transaction.

If you go to *Wallets* tab and scroll down to *Latest Transactions* section, you would see a transaction entry for the above record and confirmation block counts (0 of 12.). To invoke this transaction, the miner needs to be started, as they would execute the transaction and commit the block. Start the miner again in the *geth sub-console* using the command *miner.start(2)* as described earlier and you would see the confirmation block count progressively increasing as shown in the figure below.

Once the confirmation count reaches 12 of 12, the block would be added to the blockchain. If you click on it, you can view the transaction details and block number mined for this transaction.

Note – The number of confirmations is the number of new blocks (in a sequence) that is appended to a block of transaction. The 12 number implies, 12 new blocks were appended to the block that contains your transaction. Once the confirmation is reached, the transaction block is committed. The confirmation is required to ensure a secure block is being committed to the blockchain and avoid orphaned blocks. The orphaned block occurs when two miners produce blocks at the same time. However, some public Ethereum network might require many blocks for confirmation based on their use cases, which implies it might even take hour(s) for a single block to be committed. For more details, refer to this excellent article from Vitalik Buterin at https://blog.ethereum.org/2015/09/14/on-slow-and-fast-block-times/

Similarly, create another account called *Funder2* and transfer 500 ethers from *Main Account*. For the beneficiary account, create an account and call it as *ProjectAI*. We will transfer the funds to *ProjectAI* account now using smart contract. Copy the address of *ProjectAI* account, as we would need this later once we deploy the contract. The following image shows the snapshot of all the accounts created so far along with its balance in ethers.

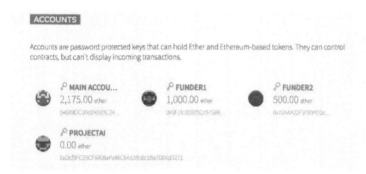

Creating and Deploying Smart Contract

In this section, we would implement and deploy the smart contract for our use case.

The crowdsourcing contract is in ethereum/contract folder. Open the *CrowdSourceContract.sol* file. We will go over the important code snippets of our contract. Our contract is written in Solidity programming language. There are three main components to look at:

CrowdFunding - This is the contract class.

FundingProject – A custom type that hold project details as part of the contract.

Funder – A custom type that holds funder details as part of the contract.

Let's walkthrough the code:

We first specify the Solidity version required to compile our contract.

```
pragma solidity ^0.4.11;
```

We then create the *CrowdFunding* contract using the *contract* keyword

```
contract CrowdFunding {
```

The *CrowdFunding* contract contains the *FundingProject* and *Funder* custom types with required attributes. We then create instances of the custom types.

```
//Funding project details
  struct FundingProject {

      string name;
      string email;
      string website;
      uint minimumfunds;
      uint amountraised;
      address owner;
      string status;

  }

  //Funder who funds project.
  struct Funder {
      string name;
      address fundedby;
      uint amount;
  }

  //Multiple funders can fund project
```

```
Funder[] public funders;

//Instance
FundingProject public fundingproject
```

Next, we define methods/operations that would be exposed by our contract.

The *CrowdFunding()* method shown below is the constructor of our contract which would initialize the project details. It expects parameters that are used to initialize the *FundingProject* type. We will show you how to pass these parameters once we instantiate the contract through our wallet interface in the next section.

```
function CrowdFunding (
    string _name,
    string _email,
    string _website,
    uint _minimumfunds,
    address _owner
    )
{

//convert to ether
uint minimumfunds = _minimumfunds * 1 ether;
uint amountraised = 0;
fundingproject =
FundingProject(_name,_email,_website,
minimumfunds,amountraised,_owner,
"Funding Started");

}
```

Next, we initialize the *Funder* type and assign it to the *funders* array as part of the *fundProject()* method. The attribute *amountraised* of the *FundingProject* type will be updated to reflect the funder's amount. It means the funder has provided funding of that amount value. If the attribute *amountraised* is greater than *minimumfunds* i.e. if the project meets the funding target then the amount is sent to the beneficiary account named *ProjectAl*. This is done using the *send()* method of the *FundingProject.owner* attribute. Following shows the code snippet -

```
fundingproject.owner.send(fundingproject.amountraised)
```

The important thing to note is that the amount reaches the ProjectAl account only when minimum funding amount is raised. Until that duration, the amount transferred from Funder's account is put on hold by the contract.

The below *fundProject*() method uses the payable modifier to receive ethers from the application (i.e., from Funders account who is funding the project)

```
function fundProject( string name) public payable {

if (stringsEqual(fundingproject.status ,"Funding Completed")) revert();
        funders.push(Funder({
                        name: name,
                        fundedby: msg.sender,
                        amount: msg.value
                })
            );
        fundingproject.amountraised =
        fundingproject.amountraised + msg.value ;

if (fundingproject.amountraised >=
        fundingproject.minimumfunds) {
```

```
        if(!fundingproject.owner.send(fundingproject.amountraised ))
revert();
        fundingproject.status = "Funding Completed";
        }
        else {
                fundingproject.status = "In Progress";
        }
}
```

Next, we define the *stopFundRaising()* method. The said method returns all the money to the respective Funders (if the funding target is not met) by iterating through the funders array and calling the *send()* method of *Funder.fundedBy* attribute for each funder object in the array. Following shows the code snippet -

```
funders[p].fundedby.send(funders[p].amount)
```

The *stopFundRaising()* method uses the *payable* modifier to send ethers from the contract to respective funders account.

```
function  stopFundRaising() public payable {
        if (stringsEqual(fundingproject.status ,"Funding Completed"))
revert();
        fundingproject.status = "Funding Stopped";
        //return money to all funders
        for (uint p = 0; p < funders.length; p++) {
                if(!funders[p].fundedby.send(funders[p].amount)) throw;
        }
        fundingproject.amountraised = 0;
   }
```

Next, we define the *getProjectStatus()* constant method, that displays the status of the project at any interval.

```
function getProjectStatus() public constant        returns(string) {
                return (fundingproject.status);
```

}

We now have our *CrowdFunding* contract ready, the next step will be to deploy the same. You can copy the content of the CrowdSourceContract.sol file and navigate back to Ethereum Wallet application. Click on *Contracts* from the top menu. On contracts window, navigate to *Deploy New Contract*. Select *Main Account* as the *From* option.

Paste the copied content inside the *Solidity Contract Source code* window. The resulting contract will be converted to bytecode once it is successfully compiled. If there were an error in the contract, you would see a message "could not compile source code."

Once the contract is compiled successfully, select the contract *Crowd Funding* from *Select Contract to Deploy* dropbox as shown in the figure below and enter the following details:

- Enter name as ProjectAI
- Enter any email address and website
- For minimum funds, enter 1000. This is the minimum amount to be raised for this crowdfunding project.
- Enter the address of account ProjectAI (if you recall, we had copied and saved this earlier)
- Click *Deploy*

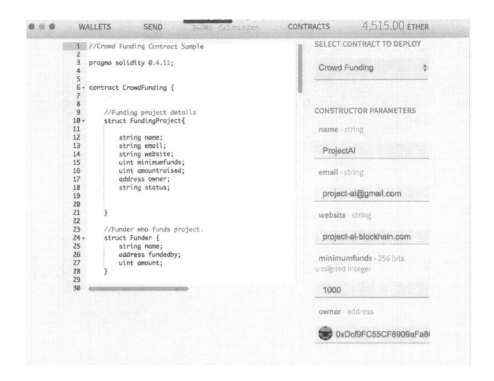

```
1  //Crowd Funding Contract Sample
2
3  pragma solidity 0.4.11;
4
5
6 ▾ contract CrowdFunding {
7
8
9      //Funding project details
10 ▾   struct FundingProject{
11
12        string name;
13        string email;
14        string website;
15        uint minimumfunds;
16        uint amountraised;
17        address owner;
18        string status;
19
20
21    }
22
23     //Funder who funds project.
24 ▾   struct Funder {
25        string name;
26        address fundedby;
27        uint amount;
28    }
29
30
```

SELECT CONTRACT TO DEPLOY

Crowd Funding ⇕

CONSTRUCTOR PARAMETERS

name - string

ProjectAI

email - string

project-ai@gmail.com

website - string

project-ai-blockhain.com

minimumfunds - 256 bits
unsigned integer

1000

owner - address

⬤ 0xDcf9FC55CF6909aFa8

On the *Create contract* window, you would see the transaction fee and gas price for deploying the contract as shown in the figure below. Enter the password of the *Main Account* and click *Send Transaction.*

If you go to *Wallets* tab and scroll down to the *Latest Transactions* section, you would see "Crowdsourcing Contract" being committed. Once all the confirmations are done, click on the transaction entry. You would see the transaction details and public address of the contract in the *To* column as shown in the figure below.

Click on the *Crowd Funding* public address link, and you would see the contract details. You can verify the contract details entered earlier. You will also see the status of the project as *Funding Started* as shown in the figure below.

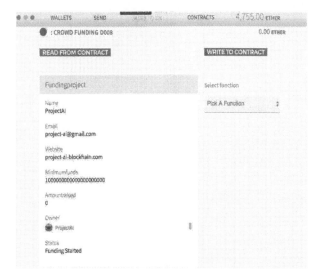

Now, in the *Select function* drop down, select *Fund Project* method and enter name as "Fund from Funder 1". In the *Execute from* option select Funder 1 and specify 700 as ether amount as shown in the figure below.

Click Execute. On the Execute Contract window, specify the password for *Funder1* and click *Send Transaction*. You should see the amount raised as 700000000000000000000 and status of the project changed as "In progress." The 700000000000000000000 value is in wei units (1 Ether = 1000000000000000000 wei), the Wallet displays currency in wei units. You can verify the transaction details in the *Latest Transaction* view, and you should also see 700 ethers and transaction fee deducted from the *Funder1* balance.

Next, go back to the contract (either by clicking on contract link from the transaction view or by selecting *Contracts* from the top menu and clicking on the specific contract address from the custom contract list).

Now, select *Fund Project* method from *Select function* dropdown and this time, select *Funder2* and transfer 350 ethers as shown below.

Click *Execute* and send the transaction. Once the transaction is committed, you will see the status of the project changed to Funding Completed. You should also see 350 ethers and transaction fee deducted from the *Funder2* balance. The *ProjectAI* account would be credited with 1050 ether amount.

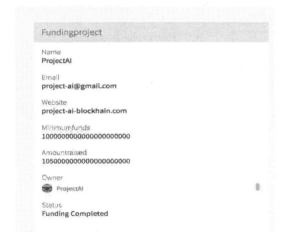

Next, we would execute the Stop Funding use case, where the amount funded by Funders would be transferred back to the Funders wallet if the funding target is not met.

For this use case, we would follow similar steps as described earlier with the addition of executing the Stop Funding function. Let's call this as Use Case 2 (we would reference this later). To implement 'Stop Funding' use case, carry out the following steps :

1. Create a new contract as per earlier guidelines and copy the content of CrowdFunding.sol in the new contract
2. Select *Crowd Funding* contract and provide the necessary details. Provide minimum funds as 500 and execute the contract.
3. Verify the project status as 'Funding Started'.
4. Select the *Fund Project* method and transfer 200 ethers from *Funder1 account*. Execute the transaction.
5. Verify the minimum funding amount value is 200 for this project after the transaction is executed.
6. Now, execute the *Stop Fund Raising* method, select the *execute* from as *Main Account (or Funder1 Account)*. Click *Execute*.
7. The status of the project would be *Funding Stopped,* and you will see the 200 Ether transferred back to *Funder1 Account*. You can verify the balance of the Funder1 *Account*.

Interacting with the Contract using Web App

In this section, we would create a front-end web application that would execute our smart contract. As mentioned earlier, the DApp comprises of a frontend and a blackened code. We implemented the backend code for our crowdsourcing application using smart contract. Now, to interact with the smart contract and the blockchain network using a frontend application, we have a wide range of options. You can develop using the Web3.js JavaScript library or install a framework like Truffle that provides a development and testing environment for building DApp.

For our use case, we would use the Web3.js library to interact with our smart contract. We will execute the same steps we carried out in Use Case 2, but this time, we would call the Stop Fund Raising method of the contract through the user interface and check the status of the project once the block has been committed to our local blockchain network.

To get started, carry out steps 1 -5 as listed in Use Case 2 as a prerequisite. Next, navigate to ethereum/web folder of the downloaded source code location and open the home.html in any editor. Let's look at some of the important code snippets.

In home.html, we first add web3.js library.

```
<script type="text/javascript" src="web3.js"></script>
```

Next, we specify the public address of the contract. Replace the below address with the address of the contract you created for this use case. (Tip: Click on the newly created contract address in Ethereum Wallet and select *copy address* on the contract page)

```
var contract_address =
"0x0EfBae3f8e3bc34b4A77E07c75dFd9f9A32f6bA2";
```

Next, we will initialize a variable with the contract details in JSON format. To get these details, click the *Show Interface* icon, as shown below, on the contract page and you will the relevant contract information in JSON format.

Contract JSON Interface

[{ "constant": true, "inputs": [],
"name": "fundingproject", "outputs":
[{ "name": "name", "type": "string",
"value": "ProjectAI" }, { "name":
"email", "type": "string", "value":
"project-ai@gmail.com" }, { "name":
"website", "type": "string", "value":
"project-ai-blockhain.com" }, {
"name": "minimumfunds", "type":
"uint256", "value": "1e+21" }, {

If you want to have someone else execute this
contract, send this information along with the
contract's address.

We have defined the contract_abi variable and initialized it with the above contract details.

```
var contract_abi = [ { "constant": true, "inputs": [], "name": "fundingproject",
"outputs": [ { "name": "name", "type": "string", "value": "g" }, { "name":
"email", ….. "payable": false, "type": "constructor" } ]
```

Next, we create the Web3 instance by providing the endpoint address of our running Ethereum instance.

```
web3 = new Web3(new
Web3.providers.HttpProvider("http://127.0.0.1:8545"));
```

Next, we create the instance of contract by providing the contract details as part of contract_abi variable and address of the contract.

```
var contract_instance = web3.eth.contract(contract_abi).at(contract_address);
```

In our HTML page, we have added a button named *Stop Fund Raising*, once clicked will invoke the *getStatus()* method. The *getStatus()* method calls the *stopFundRaising()* method on the contract instance. To execute the operations on the contract, we also provide the account (the Main Account for this example), which would pay the transaction fee to execute this transaction on the blockchain network. While running this, replace the *'passw0rd'* value in the *unlockAccount* method below, with the password of your Main account.

The following shows the *getStatus()* method.

```
function getStatus() {

//Unlock main Ether Base account and replace password with your account
password
//This is a demo setup only, get this value through secured login credentials
in actual environment
        web3.personal.unlockAccount(web3.eth.accounts[0], 'passw0rd');
//Call the Stop Fund Raising method
        contract_instance.stopFundRaising({from: web3.eth.accounts[0]},
function(error, result) {
            if(error) {
                console.error(error);
            } else {
                var hash = result;
                console.log("hash"+hash);
                checkHashStatus(hash, updateStatusFromContract);
            }
        });
    }
```

Now, once the *stopFundRaising* method is executed, the transaction will be committed as a block in the blockchain network. As we are running this on the local network, it shouldn't take more than a minute or so to execute. To track the transaction, we will store the returned hashed value of the submitted transaction. We then call the *getTransactionReceipt()* method passing the hash value as a parameter. The said method will be invoked recursively every one minute to check for the valid returned object. If the method returns a valid object, it implies the block is committed, and the transaction is complete. The following code snippet shows the *checkHashStatus()* which makes a call to the *getTransactionReceipt()* of the web3 API:

```
function checkHashStatus(hash, callback) {
web3.eth.getTransactionReceipt(hash, function(error, rcpt) {
        if(error) {
            console.error(error);
        } else {
            if(rcpt == null) {
                setTimeout(function() {
//call iteratively till hash matches and block is mined
                checkHashStatus(hash, callback);
            }, 1000);
            } else {
                console.log(rcpt)
                //call the function once block is committed
                callback();
            }
        }
    })
}
```

We also print the response from the *getTransactionReceipt()* method on the browser console, and you can verify the hash, block number, address (contract address) and other details like gas used for this transaction.

{blockHash: "0x739f8a73aa5e7ccca62be65d2f43be732c82ac02693d298ce2af64354be9ee1b", blockNumber: 39659, contractAddress: null, cumulativeGasUsed: 32083, from:

"0x6b8dc00c09dd3c240c0b964ccec6baf07ab038a5", to:"0x290298bf15d954
6850161e3046233801f2488523"...}

Once we receive the transaction receipt, we print the status of the project
on the html page as shown below. The status is fetched by invoking the
getProjectStatus() method on the contract instance. The method returns the
status as 'Funding Stopped'.

```
document.getElementById("status").innerText =
contract_instance.getProjectStatus();
```

This completes one end-to-end transaction of a web application invoking a
smart contract.

Note - The above example uses ether tokens for crowdfunding. As a next step,
you can create your own digital token for crowdfunding. You can extend the
ECR20 Token Contract
(https://theethereum.wiki/w/index.php/ERC20_Token_Standard) as the starting
point to create your own Initial Coin offering (ICO) and club it with the crowd
funding contract logic, which will use your coins for fund raising.
Investors/Participant would invest in your idea by buying your tokens with a hope
that their investment and value in tokens multiplies based on the success of the
funded project.

Extensions to Ethereum platform

In the earlier sections, we have been talking about the permissionless open
source Ethereum platform (available at https://ethereum.org/). Let's refer
to this as a Base Ethereum platform. The base Ethereum platform is good

for public related use cases where every node can participate in a transaction. However, there are other scenarios which fall outside the public-permissionless kind of use cases and therefore may require extending the Ethereum platform.

To understand this, take the example of applying the base Ethereum platform in an enterprise use case, like a complex trade finance application, which comprises of a consortium of banks, traders, sellers, government agencies and shipment vendors. For such a use case, only authorized entity/nodes are required to work together to realize a business goal. This is an example of a permissioned blockchain, where only known nodes/entity can join the network and have the ability to commit the transactions. Now, to arrive at a consensus in a permissioned blockchain, you probably need a different consensus algorithm, where a group of nodes/entity, which is accountable, provides endorsement and consensus for that transaction. For example, a trade finance blockchain network may authorize an importer bank and a buyer as endorsers of the trade terms. It means the terms cannot be deemed legal without their digital signatures.

Another aspect of the enterprise use case is the turnaround time. The time required to propose and commit the transaction should be very fast for such enterprise-level use cases. The concept of mining and solving complex mathematical equations doesn't make much sense for the permissioned network, as it's a network of known entities. Each of these entities in the permissioned network has a specific role to play and collectively work towards realizing a business goal through provenance and strong policy based consensus. For the trade finance use case, the business goal could be end-to-end visibility, accountability, secured trade, digitization, document confidentiality, automation via smart contracts and time to settlement from months to day(s).

Another aspect of enterprise use case is the ledger visibility. As there are transactions flowing throughout the network, it becomes imperative that the data is visible only between interested entities part of the business network. A simple example could be for instance, discounted product rates and terms in the trade document should not be accessible to a shipment vendor. There might be further requirements from regulations and audit side. So in short, there is a need to define a private transaction channels where only members within the channel has access to the data or ledger.

There might be many specific requirements that need to be addressed for various other use cases, which would require modifications to the base Ethereum platform or the Ethereum specification. There are many implementations available, which has extended the base Ethereum platform to provide enterprise specific capability. The following are some of the extensions:

- Quorum - Quorum is an Ethereum-based distributed ledger protocol with transaction/contract privacy and new consensus mechanisms. Quorum addresses the requirements stated above by making extensions to the base Ethereum platform.
  For more details, refer to
  https://github.com/jpmorganchase/quorum

- Hydrachain - HydraChain is an extension of the base Ethereum platform, which adds support for creating permissioned distributed ledgers through byzantine fault-tolerant consensus protocol.

- Hyperledger Burrow - Hyperledger Burrow is a permissioned Ethereum smart-contract blockchain node. For details, refer to https://github.com/hyperledger/burrow

---

Note – As blockchain being an ecosystem of business network, we are also seeing Alliances and Consortiums being formed for driving blockchain platform and implementations. For instance, The Enterprise Ethereum Alliance connects Fortune 500 enterprises, startups, academics, and technology vendors with Ethereum subject matter experts. We will see more alliances that will drive Ethereum platform to provide enterprise-grade capabilities for handling the most complex, highly demanding applications at the speed of business.

In the next chapter, we would talk about the enterprise blockchain in detail and how to build a permissioned network using HyperledgerFabric.

Smart Contract: Current and Future perspective

In this section, we will look at what applications are being developed using smart contracts, what are the current challenges and our view on the future of smart Contracts.

First, let's understand the role of smart contract. Smart contract defines and executes transactions in the form of a software code. It comprises of operations that act on the state of the blockchain ledger. So, the current capability is to manipulate and view the state in the blockchain and ensure that the shared ledger stays consistent across all the nodes in the network.

If we decide to extend the behavior of smart contract beyond just manipulating and retrieving the ledger state, like interacting with external systems for data or a third-party service, then these new requirements or extensions can impose challenges that need to be addressed. To understand this in detail, let's take an example of a DApp, where there is a requirement to read data from a public website (say stock price or forecast) as part of the smart contract functionality. Even if the data may not change in the future, how can one verify and confirm that the data received is same, genuine and unaltered throughout the network. In such a scenario, we would need a third-party system, which provides a transaction proof of the data that was accessed and retrieved at that moment. This third-party system providing secured transactions and value is referred to as oracle in blockchain terminology. So instead of smart contract accessing the public feed, the oracles extract the information and push the data into the smart contract.

Let's take another example of an existing business network or multiple networks, already having its own set of enterprise data maintained in a data store like relational databases or some legacy systems. How it can leverage blockchain technology for trust, visibility and speedy settlement and how smart contract can play a role here? Do we end up replacing legacy systems to make it work with the blockchain network or do we find out a way to achieve consensus on the existing enterprise data without replacing old systems?

To understand this, let's take an example of a trade finance application where multiple entities like banks (consortium of importer and exporter banks), shipment and logistic firms, custom/port authorities, buyers and sellers - all maintaining their own respective systems. They are looking to form a consortium of a trade finance network with the objective to devise a common smart contract that can be made accessible and visible to all the entities along with enforcing trust and speedy settlement.

In order to realize this use case, each system would need to provide their respective data in the form of attributes (we will refer to this as shared business attributes) which is essential for trade to happen. Think of shared business attributes as a common schema definition for a trade, where each entity owns and provides their respective data and make updates to it. The smart contract would then be bootstrapped with shared business attributes from each system. Each entity based on where they are in the trade process, would make necessary state changes to the smart contract and update the ledger and their respective backend systems. For example, once the goods are delivered, the shipment vendor would need to update their backend system, say a SAP application (for their actual processing and reporting). In order for the external application to receive data or attributes value via smart contract, it needs to listen to the events generated from the blockchain network (say order received event) and accordingly make updates to their backend system.

So, in a nutshell, the current generation of smart contracts and its use cases would be around providing shared business attributes that will be visible to all the concerned entities, while the rest of the functionality would still happen in their respective systems (like SAP, CRM or Mainframe system). The smart contracts of today would need to work in tandem with external systems, be it a SAP or a bank legacy application and not to replace existing systems.

In the future as blockchain platforms and smart contract technology evolves, we envision a seamless integration between smart contracts and the external systems. Most importantly the application integration should not break the consensus and therefore there is a need to create a secured environment (using crypto materials) that can seamlessly communicate with external systems. We will refer to this as an 'external contract container' responsible for integrating with the outside world. As we dwell deeper into this integration scenario, it might also make sense that the 'external contract container' should not run on all the nodes. For example, the shipment entity or node updating its SAP system need to happen only once and not by all the nodes (other participants of the blockchain network). So we are looking at only certain nodes, which are authorized based on their roles, running the 'external contract container' to communicate with external systems. We provided only one integration scenario, but there would be many such integrations patterns emerging in the future.

As you see the function of smart contract will evolve in future to cater to many such requirements, we are probably looking at the first generations of blockchain smart contract technology. We also envision new blockchain platforms with new consensus algorithms addressing external application integration using smart contract technologies and many more innovations in this space that will enable the business and consumer networks perform business with trust and transparency as part of next generation internet applications.

To conclude this section, the golden rule for any blockchain transaction is that it should be deterministic in nature. Using smart contracts allows us to manipulate the state in the blockchain in a consistent way. This is ideal for any use cases, which require shared visibility and trust across parties, where collaboration happens through an automated workflow and updates to the blockchain state is handled by smart contracts.

Summary

In this chapter, we provided a detailed overview of Ethereum and its core components. We went through a step-by-step approach of building a DApp and deploying it in the local Ethereum node. We also covered the need for extending the Ethereum platform for various use cases. At the end, we touched upon some of the current challenges of smart contract and the future implementation.

Building Blockchain applications using IBM Hyperledger Fabric

In this chapter, we will introduce a permissioned-based blockchain implementation called Hyperledger Fabric. The chapter will cover the Hyperledger Fabric component model and how to build a sample application.

Introduction to Hyperledger Fabric

Hyperledger was initiated by Linux Foundation as a base project to create blockchain based technologies. The objective of Hyperledger project is to collaboratively develop blockchain technologies through open source and community-based development. Fabric is one of the blockchain project or framework as part of Hyperledger initiative. The most distinguishing aspect of Hyperledger Fabric is that it is a permissioned-based enterprise grade blockchain platform and unlike Bitcoin or Ethereum, it does not deal with any kind of crypto-currency or mining based concept.

Hyperledger Fabric is built on four core features:

Shared Ledger - One ledger that contains transactional data and is distributed and shared across business network

Confidentiality - Controlled visibility and access to transactions through the concept of channels

Smart Contract - Business logic rules shared across the business network

Trust - All the entities in the business network own the copy of ledger and are able to verify it thereby enforcing trust

Core Component Model

In this section, we will talk about components or the building blocks of the Hyperledger Fabric framework that makes it a more complete permissioned enterprise blockchain solution.

Peer (Node)

Peer is a node in the Fabric network that performs the validation and updates to the blockchain data. A typical Fabric network will have more than one peer node in the network. It is the peer where the ledger is stored. Every peer maintains its own copy of shared ledger. A peer may also have multiple ledgers by subscribing to multiple channels (see Channel section). When transactions are delivered to the channel, it is then synced across all the peers that are part of that channel thereby keeping them in a consistent and trusted state. In a Fabric model, a peer can also perform a role of endorser where it has the ability to simulate and verify the transaction initiated by the client application. The validating peers will simply verify the transactions that were invoked making sure the data is in a consistent state before committing a block to the ledger. Fabric deployment also allows for horizontal scaling where peers can be added to the blockchain network as and when needed.

Ordering Service

Ordering service or orderer is another important component of the Fabric model. It is used to create and order blocks of transactions before it is sent to the peers for commit. All the peers receive the same block of transactions atomically and in the same order. The atomicity guarantees the network to be in the state of consensus. Once the transactions are received from the channel, the ordering service orders them according to its occurrence. It creates a chain of hashed transaction ids with each transaction pointing to the previous hashed transaction id thereby maintaining the order for that block. After the transactions are ordered, they are grouped and assigned as part of block for that channel. (See the below section for more on Channel). Client applications and peers subscribe to these channels to send or receive transactions respectively. Orderers provide two primary functionalities viz. broadcast and deliver. Broadcast is used by client applications to broadcast transactions and deliver is used by orderer to create block of these transactions and send them to peers.

Channel

Channel is a place for private communication where parties to the business network can execute transactions in a confidential way. Channels can be thought of as a partitioned topic in a messaging system where each partition acts as a separate channel, and the transactions in that partition are only visible to its subscribers. Every channel is independent of another and has its own set of security policies and chaincode (See the below section for more on Chaincode). Peers in the Fabric model must be part of a particular channel. A peer can also be part of multiple channels. Channel participants (peers) must be in the know of each other; it means that only authorized peers can be part of the channel. This is achieved using something known as genesis or the first block that contains the configuration details of the channel that states which peers can be part of this channel. One can create as many channels as needed and peers can be made part of one or more channels. Every channel will manage its own distinct ledger (transactions).

Note- The channel maps to the Ledger Conduits of our reference architecture.

Chaincode

Smart contract in Fabric model is known as chaincode. It is an application code that represents business logic to invoke transactions. Using chaincode one can read and update the ledger data. Chaincodes are executed on peers. Hyperledger Fabric provides support for Go and Java programming language for developing chaincode. When you write a chaincode, you are actually writing business logic to manipulate or query the ledger data. Chaincode must be part of the channel and can manipulate only the ledger of that channel. Peers of that channel can use one or set of multiple chaincodes to execute a complex business process workflow. Chaincode must be installed and eventually instantiated. Chaincodes are installed on every peer that forms a part of the channel. Each peer owns a copy of ledger, and therefore, chaincode must be installed on each peer for a given channel. After installation, each chaincode needs to be instantiated. Chaincode instantiation requires an endorsement policy, which suggests which peer can endorse the chaincode transaction. Every chaincode can have its own distinct policy. Policies can be customized to make it more stringent or lenient based on the business requirement.

MSP

Membership Service Provider (MSP) is one of the core components of the Fabric model that provides an abstraction over creating the identities for the network components like peers, orderers, users, etc. It provides cryptographic credentials in the form of keys and certificates that helps in authenticating and verifying network entities as they communicate with each other. It in a way provides root of trust to the blockchain network. An MSP may define its own protocol stack and rules to generate crypto credentials, which are then used for signing and verification. You could think of a business entity or an organization as one MSP. One or more MSP can be set up as part of a consortium, and the structural metadata can be provided in the configuration file. Based on the configuration, crypto materials can be generated. MSP is identified by its id and is associated with its peers and orderers in the network. Different network design topology can be thought of or devised with respect to MSP, but the usual best practice is to have one MSP per organization. One can use the cryptogen tool provided by the Fabric runtime, or you can use Fabric CA server to generate crypto artifacts like certificates and keys.

Note - The MSP maps to the abstraction level that we had talked about in Security layer of our reference architecture.

Fabric CA

Hyperledger Fabric provides a Certificate Authority (CA) component called Fabric CA, which can be used for managing the network identities of all member organizations, their nodes and users. Fabric CA drives security using cryptographically signed certificates. Every transaction whether read or update must be signed using the certificate. Fabric CA server can be used to issue certificates and associate it with different entities of the network like peer nodes or orderer nodes. It can also be used to create or register a user. If you already have users created in LDAP or Active Directory (AD), you can still use Fabric CA to integrate with your existing LDAP or AD infrastructure.

Hyperledger Fabric provides a modular architecture, so you can plug-in any CA implementation of your choice. Alternatively, you can also create your own certificates and use it as part of the blockchain network. For instance, while building the demo application later, we would use the tool called cryptogen for generating the certificates for each entity in our blockchain network.

As identity management and provenance has become a key principal of the blockchain network, Hyperledger Fabric provides an abstraction called Membership Service Provider (MSP), which provides a pluggable interface to support various identity and credential management implementations. We discussed MSP in detail in earlier section. The default implementation of MSP leverages Fabric CA component as one of the providers for identity management.

Note - The Fabric CA maps to the Certificate Authority (CA) provider that we had talked about in the security section of our reference architecture.

Working of Hyperledger Fabric

In this section, I will demonstrate the flow of a transaction from client application to the ledger. It starts with client initiating the transaction and ends with peers committing these transactions as a block to the ledger. The following steps demonstrates the transaction process flow:

Step 1: Initiating a transaction

A transaction is initiated by the client application using the command line interface (CLI) or API (like Node or Java SDK). As part of the transaction initiation process, the client sends the transaction proposal to the endorsing peers. The proposal tells the peers to invoke a transaction defined in the chaincode. This transaction proposal is appropriately signed using cryptographic credentials of the user. The following figure shows the transaction initiation process.

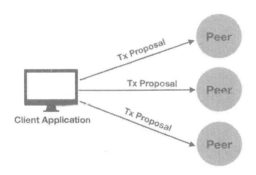

Step 2: Simulating the transaction

The endorsing peers receive the transaction proposal and verify its integrity. It checks whether the proposal was properly signed and that the client user is authorized to initiate the transaction. The endorsing peer then simulates the transaction against the ledger. Simulation is like invoking the transaction but not committing anything to the ledger yet. The output from the simulation is appropriately signed by the peers and sent back to the client application as a 'proposal response.' The following figure shows the acceptance of transaction proposal response.

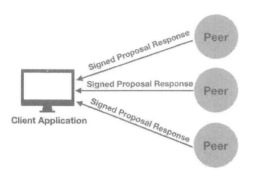

Step 3: Verifying proposal response

The client application upon receiving the proposal response verifies the same. It makes sure the signatures of the endorsing peers are valid, and the payload data is as per the expected result. It also makes sure that the transactions were endorsed as per the endorsement policy. The following figure shows the proposal response verification process.

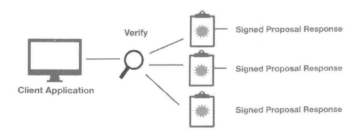

Step 4: Broadcasting transaction to the orderer

After the application client verifies the proposal response, it delivers the same, along with the proposal, to the ordering service. The delivery will be addressed to a channel by specifying the channel id. The objective of ordering service is to receive all the transaction payloads from the channel and order it in accordance with its occurrence. The ordered transactions are then put in the block. The following figure shows the transaction broadcast process.

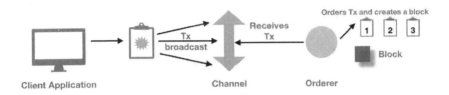

Step 5: Delivering block to Peers

The blocks created by ordering service is then delivered to the peers who are part of that channel. The peers then validate transactions. It makes sure it has followed the endorsement policy and more importantly also ensures that there is no change to the ledger state since the proposal response was created. It does so by comparing the version of the payload. The following figure shows the block delivery process.

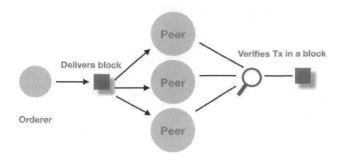

Step 6: Committing to the Ledger

Upon successful validation, each peer commits the block of transactions to the ledger. Once the ledger is updated, the status can be notified to the client application through event handling. The following figure shows the ledger commit process.

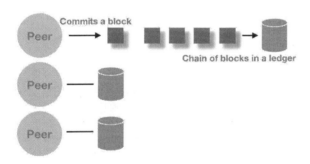

The Trade Finance Use Case

In this section, we will explore and implement the trade finance use case. Let's consider an international trade process. To carry out an international trade, several parties or organizations need to coordinate with each other.

They typically include, but not limited to: buyer (importer), seller (exporter), banks, shipping and logistics firms, port and customs authorities. The international trade process of today is often time-consuming and ineffective due to several regulations and documentation at each stage of the process. This not only makes the trade process ineffective but also adds a huge burden of cost.

Secondly, there is lack of visibility around the entire process, and each party to the trade maintains their own truth of information. There is no shared consensus and often arise lack of trust especially if they have not conducted business with each other before.

As creating the entire trading process may not be pragmatic within the scope of the book, we will implement a very simple trade finance use case that will involve exporting goods from seller to buyer and cover the process of creating and authorizing LOC and shipment using Hyperledger Fabric blockchain technology.

"Trade finance refers to financing a trade. In simple terms, a trade is an exchange of goods and services between buyers and sellers or importer and exporter. Trade can be a domestic or international trade. Banks or financial institutions provide a different form of financing avenues to support a trade. Financing does not only Involve lending money but also making sure appropriate documentation is carried out so that the trade process is efficient and parties to trade can do business with confidence and trust."

We will introduce a fictitious company named Free Trade Enterprise (FTE) - providing a trade finance application to conduct free and fair trade, transparent to all the parties. The application will be implemented using Hyperledger Fabric blockchain platform. The application will enable parties to the business execute a trade in a secured fashion by means of consensus and provenance, so as to provide transparency and accountability thereby reducing the time of financial trade from days to hours.

The FTE provides a marketplace model where trading can happen through shared consensus by the parties involved in the business. The marketplace uses many technologies apart from blockchain to make trading smooth and transparent. The technologies could include artificial Intelligence to match prospective sellers with buyers based on buyer's requirements, rating, and past trades. For new buyers, recommendation systems could pick up best-rated and safe sellers and trusted associated parties and provide optimization of trade based on similar requirements.

Internet of Thing (IoT) technology can be used to automatically track goods and shipments at various intervals. For instance, goods that require to be transported over some optimum temperature, sensors can be employed that update contracts automatically if the temperature is dropped to a certain level. GPS coordinates can be tracked at various intervals to ensure real-time event tracking of trades.

As you see the possibilities are endless and one can leverage a combination of these technologies, backed by consensus through blockchain for next generation trade platform.

The users of our trade finance application are categorized into four distinct entities:

- Buyer (registered with FTE)
- Supplier (registered with FTE)
- Importer and exporter bank (part of larger Banking Consortium)
- Shipper (Shipment and Logistics firm)

The Trade scenario

A buyer (importer) registered with FTE wishes to buy 5 cartons of rich baked almonds with each carton containing 500 packs. FTE provides a Fabric blockchain platform where parties to the trade can create relevant documentation using smart contract. The buyer initiates the process by making a purchase inquiry to the seller. The seller views the purchase order and registers a sales order against it with certain terms and conditions about the sale. Once the sale contract is established, the importer bank will issue a letter of credit (LOC) to the exporter bank. This is one way of providing credit to the buyer on presentation of relevant documents, like bill of lading, by the seller. Once the exporter bank receives and validates the terms in the letter of credit, the seller approves the same, which initiates the shipment process. The shipping company will scan the goods and prepare the bill of lading (BOL) document, signifying the initiation of shipment process. Once the buyer receives the goods, it endorses the bill of lading document thereby indicating the completion of the trade.

In the above process, we are not dealing with any physical documents like purchase order, LOC or BOL but creating a smart contract and updating the status as the trade progresses. As we move towards a digital world, we envision a future where digital contracts would replace physical documentation as legitimate and legal artifacts.

We will implement the above flow using Hyperledger Fabric and start from the LOC creation process. We will assume that buyer and the seller have entered into an agreement to perform a trade involving the purchase of rich almonds. So, our smart contract is ready with purchase and sale order details.

Application Design and Implementation strategy

We aim to provide a universal design and implementation roadmap for a permissioned-based enterprise blockchain. The stated approach is generic in nature and will provide you with a fair idea on how to kick-start your blockchain implementation in the enterprise. We will start with identifying business entities and designing the network topology and end up showing implementation and deployment. In the end, we will demonstrate the end-to-end test cases that will fulfill our smart contract as it executes transactions and query through the same to depict the final trade completion state.

The approach will have the following stages that can be used to design and implement a permissioned enterprise blockchain application:

- Defining Business Network
- Designing Network Topology
- Defining Smart Contract
- Application Deployment
- End-to-end Test Execution

Defining Business Network

Defining business network involves identifying parties to the business, their roles, and stake in the business. It involves creating users, their roles and affiliations or departments. For our trade finance application, we will use three different groups of business entities that will form the business network to carry out the trade business. All these entities will interact with the trade finance application and perform its respective function to fulfill a smart contract to take it to its logical end. In short, it will signify the completion of the trade in a free, transparent and trusted manner. The following are the three entities or organizations we will configure:

1. Free Trade Enterprise (FTE)
2. Banking Consortium (BNK)
3. Shipping and Logistics firm (SHP)

Free Trade Enterprise (FTE)

FTE will consist of registered buyers and sellers that make use of the platform to discover each other and carry out trades. Their goal will be to fulfill their purchase and sale orders respectively. They will interact with the application to typically initiate the quotations or proposal and approve them as smart contracts. The following table depicts the user organization of FTE:

User Id	Role	Organization MSP Id
User1	Buyer	Org1FTE
User2	Seller	Org1FTE

As shown in the above table, we have two users defined with the roles of buyer and seller respectively and an MSP id of the organization to which the user belongs. (Note: MSP Id can be any arbitrary value; it just identifies your organization). In Hyperledger Fabric, the users can be created using Fabric CA client component. But one can also plug in their own CA server implementation to create users or generate crypto credentials. For our trade finance application, we have used the cryptogen tool provided by Fabric runtime, to generate users and certificates. This is discussed in the later section.

Banking Consortium (BNK)

The banking consortium can be viewed as a consortium of various banks. For our trade finance application, we will have an importer and an exporter bank as a member of this consortium. Importer bank will be involved in the process of LOC creation, which will be eventually approved by the exporter bank. This will be all done using trade finance application provided by FTE through the use of smart contracts. Just like FTE, the banking consortium will also represent an MSP. The below table depicts its user organization:

User Id	Role	Organization MSP Id
User1	Importer Bank	Org2BNK
User2	Exporter Bank	Org2BNK

We will have users with the role of importer and exporter bank respectively. The MSP id of the consortium will be Org2BNK

Shipping and Logistics firm (SHP)

Our design will have a separate entity that will handle shipping and logistics aspect of the trade. Once the seller verifies the LOC approval, the shipper will initiate the shipping by creating the BOL document. This again will be done using the smart contract. The below table depicts the user organization of the shipper:

User Id	Role	Organization MSP Id
User1	Shipper	Org3SHP

There will be only one user with the role name as a shipper and the MSP id as Org3SHP

In the next stage of our design and implementation approach, we will talk about designing a network topology.

Designing Network Topology

Designing a network topology is a very significant step when it comes to implementing blockchain in the enterprise. For our trade finance application, the network topology or the deployment model will look like the following:

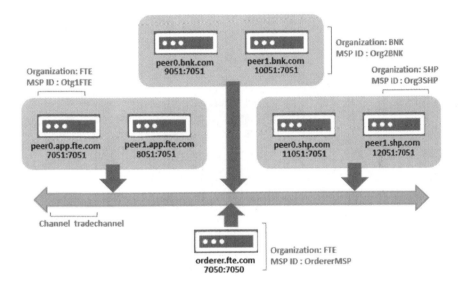

The above network topology defines a blueprint with many nodes or deployment units that communicate with each other to execute or fulfill a blockchain transaction. Our network design will comprise of six peer nodes representing three different organizations viz. FTE, BNK and SHP and an Orderer node. The model also depicts a channel that will be used by peers to validate and execute transactions.

The Orderer node will be responsible for guaranteeing transaction order and delivery. The orderer service is also used to create a channel that provides a common communication infrastructure for peer and client nodes. Our orderer node will be part of FTE organization (orderer.fte.com) hosted on port 7050. The orderer service is bootstrapped with genesis block also known as the first block of the blockchain network that contains configuration details like which organization will manage the orderer node and number of peers and users managed by each organization.

Channel is another core component that provides a common infrastructure for all the peers (part of that channel) to communicate. We will have one channel termed as 'tradechannel' where our MSP instances like orderer (orderer.fte.com) and peers from all the three organizations will participate in the transaction. Each peer will have its own copy of ledger associated with 'tradechannel' channel. In short, all the peers will have visibility of every trade finance transactions that will be carried out on this channel.

Every organization will host peer nodes. We will have two peers per each organization - peer0.app.fte.com and peer1.app.fte.com as part of FTE, peer0.bnk.com, and peer1.bnk.com as part of BNK and peer0.shp.com and peer1.shp.com as part of organization SHP. One of the responsibilities of peer is to execute the transactions and validate them against the endorsement policy. The transactions itself will be part of chaincode that represents our smart contract. And therefore, our chaincode named 'tradefinancecc' will be installed on each peer. Peers itself can also become an endorser of transactions. All the peers will form a part of channel 'tradechannel'.

In the next stage, we will talk a bit about our trade finance smart contract, termed as 'tradefinancecc'. We will explore through the business methods and workflow that will represent the trade finance application.

Defining -Smart Contract

In Fabric terminology, smart contracts are chaincodes. It has business functions that are invoked as part of transactions to query and update the state of the ledger. Our chaincode will be a smart contract termed as 'tradefinancecc'. It consists of necessary business methods that are invoked to carry out the trade finance process. Chaincodes are installed on each peer and run as an isolated docker container. The chaincode is typically stored in the *GOPATH/src* folder of your workspace. In this stage, we will walk you through each method of our smart contract and understand the trade finance application workflow. We will also look at how one can use the core chaincode interface named *ChaincodeStubInterface* to read and update the ledger state.

Before we look at each business method, let's look at the core methods of the chaincode. Every chaincode implements Chaincode interface (part of shim package) which has two core methods viz. *Init()* and *Invoke()*.

```
package main

import (
...
        "github.com/hyperledger/fabric/core/chaincode/shim"
...
)
```

As they are part of Chaincode interface, we need to import the said interface and thereby implementing *Init* and *Invoke* method. Let's look closely at the *Init* method.

The Init() method

The Init method is invoked when the chaincode is instantiated by the client application. The below code shows the Init method:

```
func (t *TradeContract) Init(stub shim.ChaincodeStubInterface) pb.Response
{
        return setupTrade(stub);
}


func setupTrade(stub shim.ChaincodeStubInterface) pb.Response {
        _, args := stub.GetFunctionAndParameters()
        tradeId := args[0]
        buyerTaxId := args[1]
        sellerTaxId := args[2]
        skuid := args[3]
        tradePrice,_ := strconv.Atoi(args[4])
        shippingPrice,_ := strconv.Atoi(args[5])

        tradeContract := trade {
                TradeId: tradeId,
                BuyerTaxId: buyerTaxId,
                SellerTaxId: sellerTaxId,
                Skuid: skuid,
                TradePrice: tradePrice,
                ShippingPrice: shippingPrice,
                Status: "Trade initiated"}

        tcBytes, _ := json.Marshal(tradeContract)
        stub.PutState(tradeContract.TradeId, tcBytes)

        return shim.Success(nil)
}
```

The Init method is passed a 'stub' object that references ChaincodeStubInterface interface. The said interface is typically used to query/update the ledger. If you recall, we mentioned earlier in this chapter that our smart contract would focus on trade finance workflow starting from LOC creation stage. It means our smart contract is already initialized with initial trade details. We have used *Init* method to initialize our trade contract with predefined values passed from the client application and fetched using *stub.GetFunctionAndParameters* method call. These values signify that the trade has reached a point where buyer and seller have agreed and accepted on the trade terms. The values reflect buyer and seller details, order and product details and more importantly, we now have a trade id. The newly initialized trade contract is then stored in the ledger using *ChaincodeStubInterface.PutState* method. Once the trade is initialized, we indicate it by returning the success status as OK.

The Invoke() method

The next core method is Invoke. The Invoke method as the name suggests will invoke our business methods. It will delegate the call to an appropriate business method based on the method name passed in the parameter. Let's look at the code below:

```
func (t *TradeContract) Invoke(stub shim.ChaincodeStubInterface)
pb.Response {
        function, args := stub.GetFunctionAndParameters()
        if function == "createLOC" {
                return t.createLOC(stub, args)
        } else if function == "approveLOC" {

                return t.approveLOC(stub, args)
        } else if function == "initiateShipment" {

                return t.initiateShipment(stub, args)
        } else if function == "deliverGoods" {
```

```
            return t.deliverGoods(stub, args)
} else if function == "shipmentDelivered" {

            return t.shipmentDelivered(stub, args)
} else if function == "query" {

            return t.query(stub, args)
}

        return shim.Error("Invalid function name")
}
```

First, we get the function name passed as an argument from the client application. This is done using *ChaincodeStubInterface.GetFunctionAndParameters()* method. Then based on the value retrieved, we invoke the appropriate business method. To sum up, the below table depicts our business methods that will fulfill our trade finance contract.

Method Name	Description	Contract State
createLOC	Importer bank creates the LOC to be sent to exporter bank. Contract is updated with the importer bank details.	LOC created
approveLOC	Exported upon seeing and verifying LOC, approves the same. Contract is updated with the exporter	LOC approved

	bank details.	
initiateShipment	The seller upon LOC approval will initiate the shipment process. The contract will update the delivery date one month from the current date.	Shipment initiated
deliverGoods	Goods are then delivered by the shipper. Contract Is updated with the shipper details.	BOL created
shipmentDelivered	Shipment is finally received by the buyer which signifies the completion of trade	Trade completed

In the next stage, we will implement our network topology as defined in stage two of the design and implementation approach.

Application Deployment

In stage two of our design and implementation approach, we showed you the network topology and the function of each network component. In this step of application deployment, we will set up this topology using Fabric based tools and commands. We will cover the whole network setup with the following steps

- Generating crypto keys and certificates
- Generating transaction configuration
- Starting the network
- Creating channel
- Joining peers to the channel
- Installing the chaincode
- Instantiating the chaincode
- Invoking the chaincode
- Querying the ledger

Generating crypto keys and certificates

The first step will be to generate keys and certificates for every organization and its associated entities like peers and orderer so that it can be used to sign/verify as they communicate over the network. For this use case, as mentioned earlier, we will use 'cryptogen' tool to generate the necessary certificates. The following command generates the x.509 based crypto files.

```
cryptogen generate --config=./crypto-config.yaml
```

The above command uses the 'cryptogen' tool that reads the 'crypto-config.yaml.' file to generate the certificates. The 'crypto-config.yaml' file depicts our network topology in a declarative way. The following configuration shows the 'crypto-config.yaml.' file that has our orderer and three organizations with peers and users.

```
OrdererOrgs:
 - Name: Orderer
   Domain: fte.com
   Specs:
    - Hostname: orderer
PeerOrgs:
```

```
- Name: Org1
  Domain: app.fte.com
  Template:
    Count: 2
  Users:
    Count: 2
- Name: Org2
  Domain: bnk.com
  Template:
    Count: 2
  Users:
    Count: 2
- Name: Org3
  Domain: shp.com
  Template:
    Count: 2
  Users:
    Count: 1
```

Peers and users are denoted by numbers (using *Count* field) where you can specify how many users and peers you would like to setup per organization.

Generating transaction configuration

Moving ahead, we will create transaction configuration artifacts. These are stated as below:

- Genesis block
- Channel transaction configuration

We will use 'configtxgen' tool to generate the above artifacts. The said tool will read the 'configtx.yaml.' file. The below configuration shows the 'configtx.yaml.' file.

```
Profiles:

    TradeFinanceOrdererGenesis:
        Orderer:
            <<: *OrdererDefaults
            Organizations:
                - *OrdererOrg
        Consortiums:
            TradeConsortium:
                Organizations:
                    - *Org1
                    - *Org2
                    - *Org3

    TradeFinanceOrgsChannel:
        Consortium: TradeConsortium
        Application:
            <<: *ApplicationDefaults
            Organizations:
                - *Org1
                - *Org2
                - *Org3

Organizations:

    - &OrdererOrg
        Name: OrdererOrg
        ID: OrdererMSP
        MSPDir: crypto-config/ordererOrganizations/fte.com/msp

    - &Org1
```

```
    Name: Org1FTE
    ID: Org1FTE
    MSPDir: crypto-config/peerOrganizations/app.fte.com/msp

    AnchorPeers:
      - Host: peer0.app.fte.com
        Port: 7051


  - &Org2
    Name: Org2BNK
    ID: Org2BNK
    MSPDir: crypto-config/peerOrganizations/bnk.com/msp
    AnchorPeers:
      - Host: peer0.bnk.com
        Port: 7051


  - &Org3
    Name: Org3SHP
    ID: Org3SHP
    MSPDir: crypto-config/peerOrganizations/shp.com/msp
    AnchorPeers:
      - Host: peer0.shp.com
        Port: 7051

Orderer: &OrdererDefaults

  OrdererType: solo
  Addresses:
    - orderer.fte.com:7050
  BatchTimeout: 5s
  BatchSize:
    MaxMessageCount: 5
    AbsoluteMaxBytes: 10 MB
    PreferredMaxBytes: 512 KB

  Kafka:
```

```
        Brokers:
            - 127.0.0.1:9092

    Organizations:

    Application: &ApplicationDefaults

    Organizations:
```

The 'configtx.yaml' file consists of profiles for ordering service and channel. The orderer profile named 'TradeFinanceOrdererGenesis' will define a consortium of our three organizations. The channel profile 'TradeFinanceOrgsChannel' will have a reference to this consortium and will also imply that all the three organization's signature will be required to create that channel.

The 'configtx.yaml' file also contains information like the path to root certificates for our three organizations, the endorsing peer with endpoint details and orderer default settings.

Genesis block

As a first step, we will create a genesis block or the first block of the transaction. It is also called a configuration block, which will describe our three peer organizations and an orderer stating their root certificates and access policies. This block will initialize the blockchain network or channel. The following command generates the genesis block

```
configtxgen -profile TradeFinanceOrdererGenesis -outputBlock ./channel-
artifacts/genesis.block
```

The above command uses ordering service profile named 'TradeFinanceOrdererGenesis' to generate 'genesis.block' file and place it in the 'channel-artifacts' folder. The 'genesis.block' file will be used to bootstrap the ordering service.

Channel transaction configuration

Next, we will generate channel transaction configuration file. This will be used to create the channel for our network. The following command generates the channel transaction configuration file.

```
configtxgen -profile TradeFinanceOrgsChannel -outputCreateChannelTx
./channel-artifacts/channel.tx -channelID tradechannel
```

The above command uses channel profile named 'TradeFinanceOrgsChannel' to generate 'channel.tx' configuration file and places it in the channel-artifacts folder. The said file will be used to create the channel.

Starting the network

We will start the network by spinning up our nodes. To start these nodes, we will use docker images provided by Fabric runtime. Docker provides a consistent environment to work with different platforms like OS/Mac/Windows. Moreover, with Docker, you could also port your application on the cloud. We will spin up the following nodes:

Note: We will only show few docker code snippets here. To view the entire code, you can download it from the GitHub at https://github.com/enterprise-blockchain-book/first-edition/blob/master/hyperledger-fabric/base/docker-trade-finance-

Node: Orderer (orderer.fte.com)

Below is the short docker snippet:

```
image: hyperledger/fabric-orderer
environment:
-
ORDERER_GENERAL_GENESISFILE=/var/hyperledger/orderer/orderer.g
enesis.block
command: orderer
volumes:
- ../channel-
artifacts/genesis.block:/var/hyperledger/orderer/orderer.genesis.block
ports:
  - 7050:7050
```

The above docker image will spin up the orderer container on port 7050. The important thing to observe is that we have bootstrapped our orderer service with the genesis block we created earlier. It means the configuration block will be created on the orderer service startup. We also specify the path to root certificates and key here.

Node: Peer0 of Org1FTE(peer0.app.fte.com)

Below is the short docker snippet:

```
image: hyperledger/fabric-peer
environment:
  - CORE_PEER_TLS_CERT_FILE=/etc/hyperledger/fabric/tls/server.crt
  - CORE_PEER_TLS_KEY_FILE=/etc/hyperledger/fabric/tls/server.key
  -
CORE_PEER_TLS_ROOTCERT_FILE=/etc/hyperledger/fabric/tls/ca.crt
command: peer node start
```

```
ports:
  - 7051:7051
```

The above docker image will spin up peer node container for the first
organization. It will use 7051 as a host and container port. It also specifies
path to crypto credentials used for signing and verification. The rest of the
peer nodes will also use the same above docker image and environment,
but each will use different host port. The below are the details of other peer
nodes:

- ✓ Org1 MSP id: Org1FTE - peer1.app.fte.com - 8051:7051
- ✓ Org2 MSP id: Org2BNK - peer0.bnk.com - 9051:7051
- ✓ Org2 MSP id: Org2BNK - peer1.bnk.com - 10051:7051
- ✓ Org3 MSP id: Org3SHP - peer0.bnk.com - 11051:7051
- ✓ Org3 MSP id: Org3SHP - peer1.bnk.com - 12051:7051

Once all the nodes are up and running, we will go ahead and create the
channel.

Creating Channel

The channel creation process reads our previously generated channel
transaction configuration artifact to create the channel. The following
command creates the channel:

```
peer channel create -o orderer.fte.com:7050 -c tradechannel -f ./channel-
artifacts/channel.tx
```

The above command reads our previously configured artifact 'channel.tx'
and creates the channel with the channel name as 'tradechannel.' The '-c'
flag is used to specify the channel name. The channel name can be any
name of your choice. The '-f' flag is used to specify the configuration file, in
this case, it is 'channel.tx' we generated using 'configtxgen' tool. The

command returns the genesis block named 'tradechannel.block.' This block file is then used to make our peer nodes join the 'tradechannel' channel.

Joining peers to the channel

Once the channel is created, the peer nodes should formally join the channel to participate in the transactions on that channel. The following command is used to onboard peers to the channel 'tradechannel'.

```
peer channel join -b tradechannel.block
```

The above command is supplied with the channel block file 'tradefinance.block' we created in the previous (create channel) command. The -b' option is used to specify the channel block file. You could be wondering where the name of the peer node is provided for joining the 'tradechannel'? The answer lies in the *CORE_PEER_ADDRESS* environment variable. You have to set this environment variable with the value of peer node address that you wish to join. Since we have 6 peer nodes, we must run this command six times and change the value of the *CORE_PEER_ADDRESS* environment to point to the correct peer node address each time we run the command. So, to join the first peer node from Org1, set the *CORE_PEER_ADDRESS* variable to the value 'peer0.app.fte.com:7051' and run the above command. You then update the environment variable to point to the second peer node of the Org1, i.e., peer1.app.fte.com:7051' and run the command. Similarly, you do this for all the peer nodes in Org2 and Org3. This way you will have all the peers now becoming part of the 'tradechannel' channel. In the next step, we will install the chaincode (smart contract) on all the peer nodes.

Installing the chaincode

We will now install our trade finance chaincode file 'tradefinancecontract.go' on every peer nodes. Peer node endorses and verifies transactions invoked using the chaincode. The following command installs the chaincode in the peer node file system:

```
peer chaincode install -n tradefinancecc -v 1.0 -p
github.com/hyperledger/fabric/examples/chaincode/go/tradecontract
```

The above command will install the chaincode which is located in the path 'github.com/hyperledger/fabric/examples/chaincode/go/tradecontract' and give it a name as 'tradefinancecc'. The path denoted is mapped to volume path on the docker container. It points to 'hyperledger-fabric/chaincode/tradecontract' folder that contains our chaincode file. The chaincode will be installed in the file system of the peer node. Peer node address can be specified by setting the *CORE_PEER_ADDRESS* environment variable as stated in the previous step. Since we have six peer nodes, you must run this command six times with each time updating the said environment variable to point to correct peer address. The '-n' option is used to provide a name to chaincode, and '-p' option is used to specify the source path of our chaincode file. In the next step, we will instantiate this chaincode.

Instantiating the chaincode

Now, the chaincode 'tradefinancecc' is installed on each peer, we will instantiate the same. Instantiating the chaincode means initializing the chaincode by invoking its init() method. The following command instantiates the chaincode:

```
peer chaincode instantiate -o orderer.fte.com:7050 -C tradechannel -n
tradefinancecc -v 1.0 -c
'{"Args":["init","FTE_2","FTE_B_1","FTE_S_1","SKU001","10000","1000
```

```
"]}' -P "OR
        ('Org1FTE.member','Org2BNK.member','Org3SHP.member')"
```

The above command instantiates the chaincode on the target peer (as mentioned in the *CORE_PEER_ADDRESS* environment variable) and launches its own isolated docker container. The command uses *Args* key field to pass the function name *'Init'* and various other parameters to initialize our trade finance smart contract. It also sets the endorsing policy by specifying which organization peers will do the endorsement. The policy is specified using '-P' option.

Invoking the chaincode

With the chaincode instantiated in earlier step, we can now invoke business methods. Invoking means calling the *'Invoke'* method of the chaincode, which then calls the appropriate business method based on the method name passed as a parameter to the command. The following command invokes the 'createLOC' method of the chaincode.

```
peer chaincode invoke -o orderer.fte.com:7050 -C tradechannel -n
tradefinancecc -c '{"Args":["createLOC","FTE_2"]}'
```

The above command invokes the *'createLOC'* method on the target peer (as mentioned in the *CORE_PEER_ADDRESS* environment variable). You can point to any peer as transactions are invoked on all peers. If you recall, every peer maintains a copy of the ledger, and therefore, all peer will execute the transaction. Once the chaincode is instantiated or any business method is invoked, it starts the chaincode containers for all the peers. The above command executes *'createLOC'* method by passing the trade id. The trade status is then updated to the ledger. In the next step, we will query the state of the ledger.

Querying the ledger

Now, since we have executed one business method named *'createLOC'*, we will check if it indeed updated the trade status. You can check the state of the ledger by giving the following command:

```
peer chaincode query -C tradechannel -n mycc -c
'{"Args":["query","FTE_2"]}'
```

The above command queries the channel by passing the trade id. The query is executed on the target peer and returns the current state of the ledger. If you view the log file of the container, you will see the trade status changed to 'LOC created.'

This ends our fourth stage of design and implementation approach. In the next stage, we will demonstrate the complete end-to-end flow, fulfilling our trade finance smart contract as test cases by running a single script file.

End-to-End Test Execution

In this section, we will execute the entire network setup and business workflow using a single script representing our test cases.

You can download the source code of the book from GitHub location – https://github.com/enterprise-blockchain-book/first-edition.git, if you haven't downloaded it yet.

Go to hyperledger-fabric folder. The following shows the structure of the hyperledger-fabric folder

```
[root@instance-3:~/hyperledger-fabric# ls -l
total 40
-rwxr-xr-x 1 root root  186 Oct  7 07:48 README.md
drwxr-xr-x 2 root root 4096 Oct  7 07:48 base
drwxr-xr-x 3 root root 4096 Oct  7 07:48 chaincode
drwxr-xr-x 2 root root 4096 Oct  7 07:48 channel-artifacts
-rw-r--r-- 1 root root 1877 Oct  7 07:48 configtx.yaml
-rw-r--r-- 1 root root  483 Oct  7 07:48 crypto-config.yaml
-rw-r--r-- 1 root root 3288 Oct  7 07:48 docker-trade-finance.yaml
drwxr-xr-x 2 root root 4096 Oct  7 07:48 scripts
-rw-r--r-- 1 root root 4888 Oct  7 07:48 tradee2e.sh
root@instance-3:~/hyperledger-fabric# 
```

- The docker file - docker-trade-finance.yaml, discussed earlier that sets up the trade finance blockchain network, resides in the root folder.
- The chaincode folder contains our trade finance chaincode - tradefinancecontract.go.
- The crypto-config.yaml, explained in Defining Network Topology section earlier, is used for generating cryptographic artifacts for our entire network.
- The script folder contains the script file script.sh, which runs the end-to-end trade finance application. The script is bootstrapped in docker-trade-finance.yaml and executed upon the network startup.
- The tradee2e.sh script is the entry point to the application, which has commands to generate certificates and execute the end-to-end trade application using docker runtime.

To start with, change directory to hyperledger-fabric and download the IBM Hyperledger platform specific binaries by using the following command

curl -SSL https://goo.gl/QM1M4b | bash

You would see a bin folder created, which contains platform-specific binaries, namely cryptogen and configtxgen which are used for generating certificates and channel artifacts respectively

Let's generate the certificates and channel artifacts for our blockchain network using the following command.

./tradee2e.sh -m generate

The generate option calls the cryptogen for generating certificates and configtxgen for channel artifacts based on our configuration file. We had explained the command and configuration earlier in Application Deployment section.

You should see the following output.

```
root@instance-3:~/hyperledger-fabric# ./tradee2e.sh -m generate
/root/hyperledger-fabric/bin/cryptogen

Generate certificates using cryptogen tool ..

app.fte.com
bnk.com
shp.com

/root/hyperledger-fabric/bin/configtxgen
.. Generating Orderer Genesis block ...
2017-10-06 15:25:45.965 UTC [common/configtx/tool] main -> INFO 001 Loading configuration
2017-10-06 15:25:45.994 UTC [common/configtx/tool] doOutputBlock -> INFO 002 Generating genesis block
2017-10-06 15:25:45.995 UTC [common/configtx/tool] doOutputBlock -> INFO 003 Writing genesis block

..Generating channel configuration transaction 'channel.tx'..
2017-10-06 15:25:46.017 UTC [common/configtx/tool] main -> INFO 001 Loading configuration
2017-10-06 15:25:46.021 UTC [common/configtx/tool] doOutputChannelCreateTx -> INFO 002 Generating new channel configtx
2017-10-06 15:25:46.021 UTC [common/configtx/tool] doOutputChannelCreateTx -> INFO 003 Writing new channel tx

root@instance-3:~/hyperledger-fabric#
```

This would generate the crypto artifacts in the crypto-config folder and channel artifacts in the channel-artifacts folder.

If you inspect the crypto-config folder, you would see "ordererOrganizations" and "peerOrganizations" folder. If you navigate to the peerOrganizations-> bnk.com and drill down to respective folders, you would see the following structure as shown below.

```
root@instance-3:~/hyperledger-fabric/crypto-config/peerOrganizations/bnk.com# ls -l
total 20
drwxr-xr-x 2 root root 4096 Oct  8 17:52 ca
drwxr-xr-x 5 root root 4096 Oct  8 17:52 msp
drwxr-xr-x 4 root root 4096 Oct  8 17:52 peers
drwxr-xr-x 2 root root 4096 Oct  8 17:52 tlsca
drwxr-xr-x 5 root root 4096 Oct  8 17:52 users
root@instance-3:~/hyperledger-fabric/crypto-config/peerOrganizations/bnk.com# cd users
root@instance-3:~/hyperledger-fabric/crypto-config/peerOrganizations/bnk.com/users# ls -l
total 12
drwxr-xr-x 4 root root 4096 Oct  8 17:52 Admin@bnk.com
drwxr-xr-x 4 root root 4096 Oct  8 17:52 User1@bnk.com
drwxr-xr-x 4 root root 4096 Oct  8 17:52 User2@bnk.com
root@instance-3:~/hyperledger-fabric/crypto-config/peerOrganizations/bnk.com/users# cd User1@bnk.com/
root@instance-3:~/hyperledger-fabric/crypto-config/peerOrganizations/bnk.com/users/User1@bnk.com# ls -l
total 8
drwxr-xr-x 7 root root 4096 Oct  8 17:52 msp
drwxr-xr-x 2 root root 4096 Oct  8 17:52 tls
root@instance-3:~/hyperledger-fabric/crypto-config/peerOrganizations/bnk.com/users/User1@bnk.com# cd msp
root@instance-3:~/hyperledger-fabric/crypto-config/peerOrganizations/bnk.com/users/User1@bnk.com/msp# ls -l
total 20
drwxr-xr-x 2 root root 4096 Oct  8 17:52 admincerts
drwxr-xr-x 2 root root 4096 Oct  8 17:52 cacerts
drwxr-xr-x 2 root root 4096 Oct  8 17:52 keystore
drwxr-xr-x 2 root root 4096 Oct  8 17:52 signcerts
drwxr-xr-x 2 root root 4096 Oct  8 17:52 tlscacerts
root@instance-3:~/hyperledger-fabric/crypto-config/peerOrganizations/bnk.com/users/User1@bnk.com/msp#
```

The msp folder contains cryptographic credentials for User1@bnk.com. The keystore folder contains the User1 private key and signcerts contains the public key certificate for verification. We pass this msp path of User1@bnk.com in our script file (script.sh) to invoke functions on behalf of this user and artifacts under this path are used for identification and verification. Similarly, for all peers and users, we have a similar configuration and are being referenced in the script.sh file.

Next, we would execute the application by running the following script:

```
./trade2e.sh -m up
```

As discussed earlier, this would set up the network using docker files and execute the script.sh file. The following shows the output of running the script

1. First, you would see channel -"tradechannel," being created as shown in the figure below.

```
2017-10-18 13:17:19.707 UTC [channelCmd] InitCmdFactory -> INFO 019 Endorser and or
derer connections initialized
2017-10-18 13:17:19.907 UTC [msp] GetLocalMSP -> DEBU 01a Returning existing local
MSP
2017-10-18 13:17:19.908 UTC [msp] GetDefaultSigningIdentity -> DEBU 01b Obtaining d
efault signing identity
2017-10-18 13:17:19.908 UTC [msp] GetLocalMSP -> DEBU 01c Returning existing local
MSP
2017-10-18 13:17:19.908 UTC [msp] GetDefaultSigningIdentity -> DEBU 01d Obtaining d
efault signing identity
2017-10-18 13:17:19.908 UTC [msp/identity] Sign -> DEBU 01e Sign: plaintext: 0AB106
0A1808021A0608DFA89DCF0522...EC8AE2F3815112080A021A0012021A00
2017-10-18 13:17:19.908 UTC [msp/identity] Sign -> DEBU 01f Sign: digest: 692993059
FC92CDB4A4E42B6945341F4356250F669DF8969CFC6E9AD76745ED0
2017-10-18 13:17:19.914 UTC [channelCmd] readBlock -> DEBU 020 Received block: 0
2017-10-18 13:17:19.915 UTC [main] main -> INFO 021 Exiting.....
Channel "tradechannel" is created successfully.
```

2. Next, all peers would join the channel one by one. The following shows peer 0 joining the network. Similar messages would be displayed for peer 1, peer 2, peer 3, peer 4 and peer 5.

```
CORE_PEER_TLS_ENABLED=true
CORE_PEER_MSPCONFIGPATH=/opt/gopath/src/github.com/hyperledger/fabric/peer/crypto/p
eerOrganizations/app.fte.com/users/Admin@app.fte.com/msp
CORE_PEER_ID=cli
CORE_LOGGING_LEVEL=DEBUG
CORE_PEER_ADDRESS=peer0.app.fte.com:7051
2017-10-18 13:17:19.960 UTC [msp] GetLocalMSP -> DEBU 001 Returning existing local
MSP
2017-10-18 13:17:19.960 UTC [msp] GetDefaultSigningIdentity -> DEBU 002 Obtaining d
efault signing identity
2017-10-18 13:17:19.963 UTC [channelCmd] InitCmdFactory -> INFO 003 Endorser and or
derer connections initialized
2017-10-18 13:17:19.964 UTC [msp/identity] Sign -> DEBU 004 Sign: plaintext: 0AF506
0A5C08011A0C08DFA89DCF0510...29ABF45661A41A080A000A000A000A00
2017-10-18 13:17:19.964 UTC [msp/identity] Sign -> DEBU 005 Sign: digest: 9324F3808
E7A24121D4E33E694D4D5F1E345E2CE884DF7BDF896C005D3CA0F9F
2017-10-18 13:17:20.004 UTC [channelCmd] executeJoin -> INFO 006 Peer joined the ch
annel!
2017-10-18 13:17:20.004 UTC [main] main -> INFO 007 Exiting.....
PEER0 joined on the channel "tradechannel".
```

3. Next, the chain code would be deployed on all peers. You would see a message – "Chaincode is installed on remote peer." The following shows the message for peer 0.

```
2017-10-18 13:17:44.849 UTC [golang-platform] func1 -> DEBU 007 Discarding GOROOT p
ackage fmt
2017-10-18 13:17:44.849 UTC [golang-platform] func1 -> DEBU 008 Discarding provided
 package github.com/hyperledger/fabric/core/chaincode/shim
2017-10-18 13:17:44.849 UTC [golang-platform] func1 -> DEBU 009 Discarding provided
 package github.com/hyperledger/fabric/protos/peer
2017-10-18 13:17:44.849 UTC [golang-platform] func1 -> DEBU 00a Discarding GOROOT p
ackage strconv
2017-10-18 13:17:44.849 UTC [golang-platform] func1 -> DEBU 00b Discarding GOROOT p
ackage time
2017-10-18 13:17:44.849 UTC [golang-platform] GetDeploymentPayload -> DEBU 00c done
2017-10-18 13:17:44.852 UTC [msp/identity] Sign -> DEBU 00d Sign: plaintext: 0AF506
0A5C08031A0C08F8A89DCF0510...9732FE080000FFFF9669F3E6001E0000
2017-10-18 13:17:44.852 UTC [msp/identity] Sign -> DEBU 00e Sign: digest: EA778C8A7
3CA34167979615DF3BE7E03F1A46CA5DF0D152B2B6B1A3EE1899B7C
2017-10-18 13:17:44.856 UTC [chaincodeCmd] install -> DEBU 00f Installed remotely r
esponse:<status:200 payload:"OK" >
2017-10-18 13:17:44.856 UTC [main] main -> INFO 010 Exiting.....
Chaincode is installed on remote peer PEER 0.
```

4. Next, the chain code would be instantiated on peer 1. You should see a message – "Chaincode Instantiation on PEER 1 on channel 'tradechannel' is successful."

```
Instantiating chaincode on Org1FTE/peer1.
CORE_PEER_TLS_ROOTCERT_FILE=/opt/gopath/src/github.com/hyperledger/fabric/peer/cryp
to/peerOrganizations/app.fte.com/peers/peer0.app.fte.com/tls/ca.crt
CORE_PEER_TLS_KEY_FILE=/opt/gopath/src/github.com/hyperledger/fabric/peer/crypto/pe
erOrganizations/app.fte.com/peers/peer0.app.fte.com/tls/server.key
CORE_PEER_LOCALMSPID=Org1FTE
CORE_VM_ENDPOINT=unix:///host/var/run/docker.sock
CORE_PEER_TLS_CERT_FILE=/opt/gopath/src/github.com/hyperledger/fabric/peer/crypto/p
eerOrganizations/app.fte.com/peers/peer0.app.fte.com/tls/server.crt
CORE_PEER_TLS_ENABLED=true
CORE_PEER_MSPCONFIGPATH=/opt/gopath/src/github.com/hyperledger/fabric/peer/crypto/p
eerOrganizations/app.fte.com/users/Admin@app.fte.com/msp
CORE_PEER_ID=cli
CORE_LOGGING_LEVEL=DEBUG
CORE_PEER_ADDRESS=peer1.app.fte.com:7051
2017-10-18 13:17:46.646 UTC [msp] GetLocalMSP -> DEBU 001 Returning existing local
MSP
2017-10-18 13:17:46.646 UTC [msp] GetDefaultSigningIdentity -> DEBU 002 Obtaining d
efault signing identity
2017-10-18 13:17:46.649 UTC [chaincodeCmd] checkChaincodeCmdParams -> INFO 003 Usin
g default escc
2017-10-18 13:17:46.649 UTC [chaincodeCmd] checkChaincodeCmdParams -> INFO 004 Usin
g default vscc
2017-10-18 13:17:46.650 UTC [msp/identity] Sign -> DEBU 005 Sign: plaintext: 0A8307
0A6A08031A0C08FAA89DCF0510...335348500A04657363630A0476736363
2017-10-18 13:17:46.650 UTC [msp/identity] Sign -> DEBU 006 Sign: digest: 365D53B33
EC577B39B1DE4D0CF15856D8CE84507BAF80C8CA88E0139927C308
2017-10-18 13:18:04.177 UTC [msp/identity] Sign -> DEBU 007 Sign: plaintext: 0A8307
0A6A08031A0C08FAA89DCF0510...E6B075854B3A9B983D64B8C6BFE4E5FE
2017-10-18 13:18:04.177 UTC [msp/identity] Sign -> DEBU 008 Sign: digest: 692257FDE
DBCC7B703B017B0F9B5A17752A6297F46FED0F7DD9920368A874EA3
2017-10-18 13:18:04.183 UTC [main] main -> INFO 009 Exiting.....
Chaincode Instantiation on PEER 1 on channel 'tradechannel' is successful.
```

5. Next, we would query the initial state after instantiation on different peers, say peer 2, which shows that chaincode is instantiated on all other peers as well.

```
Querying chaincode on Org2BNK/peer0.
Querying on PEER2 on channel 'tradechannel'.
CORE_PEER_TLS_ROOTCERT_FILE=/opt/gopath/src/github.com/hyperledger/fabric/peer/cryp
to/peerOrganizations/bnk.com/peers/peer0.bnk.com/tls/ca.crt
CORE_PEER_TLS_KEY_FILE=/opt/gopath/src/github.com/hyperledger/fabric/peer/crypto/pe
erOrganizations/app.fte.com/peers/peer0.app.fte.com/tls/server.key
CORE_PEER_LOCALMSPID=Org2BNK
CORE_VM_ENDPOINT=unix:///host/var/run/docker.sock
CORE_PEER_TLS_CERT_FILE=/opt/gopath/src/github.com/hyperledger/fabric/peer/crypto/p
eerOrganizations/app.fte.com/peers/peer0.app.fte.com/tls/server.crt
CORE_PEER_TLS_ENABLED=true
CORE_PEER_MSPCONFIGPATH=/opt/gopath/src/github.com/hyperledger/fabric/peer/crypto/p
eerOrganizations/bnk.com/users/Admin@bnk.com/msp
CORE_PEER_ID=cli
CORE_LOGGING_LEVEL=DEBUG
CORE_PEER_ADDRESS=peer0.bnk.com:7051
Attempting to Query PEER2 ...4 secs
Attempting to Query PEER2 ...8 secs
Attempting to Query PEER2 ...29 secs
Attempting to Query PEER2 ...33 secs
Attempting to Query PEER2 ...37 secs
Attempting to Query PEER2 ...41 secs
Attempting to Query PEER2 ...45 secs
Attempting to Query PEER2 ...49 secs
Attempting to Query PEER2 ...54 secs
Attempting to Query PEER2 ...58 secs
Attempting to Query PEER2 ...62 secs

2017-10-18 13:19:06.209 UTC [msp] GetLocalMSP -> DEBU 001 Returning existing local
MSP
2017-10-18 13:19:06.209 UTC [msp] GetDefaultSigningIdentity -> DEBU 002 Obtaining d
efault signing identity
2017-10-18 13:19:06.210 UTC [chaincodeCmd] checkChaincodeCmdParams -> INFO 003 Usin
g default escc
2017-10-18 13:19:06.210 UTC [chaincodeCmd] checkChaincodeCmdParams -> INFO 004 Usin
g default vscc
2017-10-18 13:19:06.210 UTC [msp/identity] Sign -> DEBU 005 Sign: plaintext: 0AF806
0A7308031A0B08CAA99DCF0510...1A0E0A057175657279890A054654455F32
2017-10-18 13:19:06.210 UTC [msp/identity] Sign -> DEBU 006 Sign: digest: F35FF8AB7
B39B2DFD66BD2B30C73061CB06EED7DE5A4B169CEE7C16F00E795FC
Query Result: {"TradeId":"FTE_2","BuyerTaxId":"FTE_B_1","Skuid":"SKU001","SellerTax
Id":"FTE_S_1","ExportBankId":"","ImportBankId":"","DeliveryDate":"","ShipperId":"",
"Status":"Trade initiated","TradePrice":10000,"ShippingPrice":1000}
2017-10-18 13:19:06.216 UTC [main] main -> INFO 007 Exiting....
```

6. Next, we would execute the *createLOC* command using importer bank user (i.e., User1@bnk.com). Following shows the output of invocation. A successful message stating –" Invoke:createLOC transaction on PEER PEER2 on channel 'tradechannel' is successful." should be printed.

```
invoke result: version:1 response:<status:200 message:"OK" > payload:"\n s\250\253y
YD\333\3115F7`\037\220\313-\312\025\341\013\222\353f\366\000\325\354i\267\026\364l\
022\315\002\n\256\002\022\036\n\004lscc\022\026\n\024\n\016tradefinancecc\022\002\0
10\001\022\213\002\n\016tradefinancecc\022\370\001\n\013\n\005FTE_2\022\002\010\001
\032\350\001\n\005FTE_2\032\336\001{\"TradeId\":\"FTE_2\",\"BuyerTaxId\":\"FTE_B_1\
",\"Skuid\":\"SKU001\",\"SellerTaxId\":\"FTE_S_1\",\"ExportBankId\":\"\",\"ImportBa
nkId\":\"BNK_I_1\",\"DeliveryDate\":\"\",\"ShipperId\":\"\",\"Status\":\"LOC create
d\",\"TradePrice\":10000,\"ShippingPrice\":1000}\032\003\010\310\001\"\025\022\016t
radefinancecc\032\0031.0" endorsement:<endorser:"\n\0070rg2BNK\022\333\005-----BEGI
N -----\nMIIB/jCCAaWgAwIBAgIRAN3NRCdLO5xttpv1UyFeiGwwCgYIKoZIzj0EAwIwYTEL\nMAkGA1UE
BhMCVVMxEzARBgNVBAgTCkNhbGlmb3JuaWExFjAUBgNVBAcTDVNhbiBG\ncmFuY2lzY28xEDAOBgNVBAoTB
2Juay5jb20xEzARBgNVBAMTCmNhLmJuay5jb20w\nHhcNMTcxMDE4MTMxMjE1WhcNMjcxMDE2MTMxMjE1Wj
BSMQswCQYDVQQGEwJVUzET\nMBEGA1UECBMKQ2FsaWZvcm5pYTEWMBQGA1UEBxMNU2FuIEZyYW5jaXNjbzE
WMBQG\nA1UEAxMNcGVlcjAuYm5rLmNvbTBZMBMGByqGSM49AgEGCCqGSM49AwEHA0IABKzt\numlbBuXJqo
PvCg1VfHenqB7HvyAQ7JpU+KYo2apqHNry5o6akky2h5914LRNVySV\nzIh2lZDCZxEiEpcL1TGjTTBLMA4
GA1UdDwEB/wQEAwIHgDAMBgNVHRMBAf8EAjAA\nMCsGA1UdIwQkMCKAIGaNl4kEQRZEkkr8NO/qa8YvfjCe
e167GdM3YATQLAqNMAoG\nCCqGSM49BAMCA0cAMEQCIH+/UhzjD6qWKC3DQbzmfyZZgxmwLikPfJ2PPOO8u
o4E\nAiBzQoSNslRMyCsOPvrfxEmNiWM2/qizQhR5rvmiH+19ww==\n-----END -----\n" signature:
"0E\002!\000\217p\265'\321\261\211\351\376\243\337\032Q-\013\016\307\321\032\374\31
0L\374\213%E\213\242\352\017\204\010\002 \027y\002Z\311\036~\321\342w\031\032i\205\
342H\322\037S\037\030l\017\346\302s\233\0218#\3539"
2017-10-18 13:19:06.283 UTC [chaincodeCmd] chaincodeInvokeOrQuery -> INFO 00a Chain
code invoke successful. result: status:200
2017-10-18 13:19:06.284 UTC [main] main -> INFO 00b Exiting.....
Invoke:createLOC transaction on PEER PEER2 on channel 'tradechannel' is successful.
```

7. Next, we execute the *approveLOC* method using User2@bnk.com (exporter bank), *initiateShipment* method using User2@app.fte.com (Seller) , *deliverGoods* method using User1@shp.com (Shipment Org user) and *shipmentDelivered* method using User1@app.fte.com (Buyer). After every method invocation, we query the ledger to verify the trade status.

8. At the final step, we query the status of the trade, which shows the expected output as 'Trade completed" as shown below.

```
2017-10-18 13:25:04.747 UTC [msp/identity] Sign -> DEBU 005 Sign: plaintext: 0A8D07
0A7408031A0C08B0AC9DCF0510...1A0E0A0571756572790A054654455F32
2017-10-18 13:25:04.747 UTC [msp/identity] Sign -> DEBU 006 Sign: digest: 4738216ED
B17D533DFC0DFEF53656F70CDC8CEBB601A18E73A893C8DAC5BAC36
Query Result: {"TradeId":"FTE_2","BuyerTaxId":"FTE_B_1","Skuid":"SKU001","SellerTax
Id":"FTE_S_1","ExportBankId":"BNK_E_1","ImportBankId":"BNK_I_1","DeliveryDate":"11-
18-2017","ShipperId":"SHP_1","Status":"Trade completed","TradePrice":10000,"Shippin
gPrice":1000}
2017-10-18 13:25:04.754 UTC [main] main -> INFO 007 Exiting.....

Trade Finance  End to End application completed.
```

This completes one end-to-end flow. You can also run these commands from the peer nodes by logging into the docker instance. Our trade application launches a set of docker containers. To see the list of containers spawned by the trade finance application, you can type in *docker ps* command. You would see 6 peer nodes and 1 orderer node as shown below. You will also see chaincode containers prefixed with 'dev.' As we had mentioned earlier in the previous section, chaincode, once instantiated, runs in its own isolated environment as a docker container.

```
[root@instance-3:~# docker ps
CONTAINER ID        IMAGE
                                          COMMAND                     CREATED
  STATUS            PORTS                                             NAMES
16dc6b7d0949        dev-peer0.shp.com-tradefinancecc-1.0-9ebdf3f57c95216b22e507eab4ec6
bc21c3e65fa1a5022c91042f30959c97c71       "chaincode -peer.a..."      2 hours ago
  Up 2 hours                                                          dev-peer0.shp.
com-tradefinancecc-1.0
e0d5f31a06af        dev-peer0.app.fte.com-tradefinancecc-1.0-6b610ecfa91ac6ea799eb9a96
bb3b5577f3aa6f00fd50bddaa661da6adb8223b   "chaincode -peer.a..."      2 hours ago
  Up 2 hours                                                          dev-peer0.app.
fte.com-tradefinancecc-1.0
2a38a9b2f468        dev-peer1.shp.com-tradefinancecc-1.0-4216116f82909a286545cc3c10556
bf2f21fee1a4a4e02f7cd7e759d49f063e3       "chaincode -peer.a..."      2 hours ago
  Up 2 hours                                                          dev-peer1.shp.
com-tradefinancecc-1.0
6b0ad7a6e076        dev-peer1.bnk.com-tradefinancecc-1.0-8746c5dbc6966345179a461c28943
6c8730e583b0bae577ac93636df5d481a60       "chaincode -peer.a..."      2 hours ago
  Up 2 hours                                                          dev-peer1.bnk.
com-tradefinancecc-1.0
6f188d5578c0        dev-peer0.bnk.com-tradefinancecc-1.0-9cd89a52e6be2ec5188a86ff0c050
97e726be464e6178e7e935393b2fd7eb20c       "chaincode -peer.a..."      2 hours ago
  Up 2 hours                                                          dev-peer0.bnk.
com-tradefinancecc-1.0
5e8a46e95655        dev-peer1.app.fte.com-tradefinancecc-1.0-bdc67c37324d7e46a13c60346
7481dff18541b9ab6ace05597e09b32c26b25be   "chaincode -peer.a..."      2 hours ago
  Up 2 hours                                                          dev-peer1.app.
fte.com-tradefinancecc-1.0
cd984e81c809        hyperledger/fabric-tools
                                          "/bin/bash -c './s..."      2 hours ago
  Up 2 hours                                                          cli
9d61a7b5a542        hyperledger/fabric-peer
                                          "peer node start"           2 hours ago
  Up 2 hours        0.0.0.0:8051->7051/tcp, 0.0.0.0:8053->7053/tcp    peer1.app.fte.
com
022ddcced101        hyperledger/fabric-peer
                                          "peer node start"           2 hours ago
  Up 2 hours        0.0.0.0:9051->7051/tcp, 0.0.0.0:9053->7053/tcp    peer0.bnk.com
5e7705c39850        hyperledger/fabric-peer
                                          "peer node start"           2 hours ago
```

Log in to one of the containers, say peer1.app.fte.com using its container id by executing the following command

```
docker exec -i -t 022ddcced101 /bin/bash
```

(Replace 022ddcced101 by your container id)

Once logged in, you would see the prompt -
/opt/gopath/src/github.com/hyperledger/fabric/peer

Type in the following query command to query the latest state of the ledger based on the trade id –

```
peer chaincode query -C tradechannel -n tradefinancecc -c
'{"Args":["query","FTE_2"]}'
```

You would see the query being printed on the console. The following figure shows the details.

```
root@instance-3:~# docker exec -i -t 022ddcced101 /bin/bash
root@022ddcced101:/opt/gopath/src/github.com/hyperledger/fabric/peer# peer chaincode q
uery -C tradechannel -n tradefinancecc -c '{"Args":["query","FTE_2"]}'
2017-10-18 14:58:24.453 UTC [msp] GetLocalMSP -> DEBU 001 Returning existing local MSP
2017-10-18 14:58:24.453 UTC [msp] GetDefaultSigningIdentity -> DEBU 002 Obtaining defa
ult signing identity
2017-10-18 14:58:24.453 UTC [chaincodeCmd] checkChaincodeCmdParams -> INFO 003 Using d
efault escc
2017-10-18 14:58:24.453 UTC [chaincodeCmd] checkChaincodeCmdParams -> INFO 004 Using d
efault vscc
2017-10-18 14:58:24.454 UTC [msp/identity] Sign -> DEBU 005 Sign: plaintext: 0AFD060A7
408031A0C0B90D89DCF0510...1A0E0A0571756572790A054654455F32
2017-10-18 14:58:24.454 UTC [msp/identity] Sign -> DEBU 006 Sign: digest: 94E76E0F42D9
5498348FF683AEE8546048416F2D6D4255A161FB497D7F533333
Query Result: {"TradeId":"FTE_2","BuyerTaxId":"FTE_B_1","Skuid":"SKU001","SellerTaxId"
:"FTE_S_1","ExportBankId":"BNK_E_1","ImportBankId":"BNK_I_1","DeliveryDate":"11-18-201
7","ShipperId":"SHP_1","Status":"Trade completed","TradePrice":10000,"ShippingPrice":1
000}
2017-10-18 14:58:24.466 UTC [main] main -> INFO 007 Exiting.....
root@022ddcced101:/opt/gopath/src/github.com/hyperledger/fabric/peer# 
```

Note - To stop the containers, you can run the *tradee2e* script with the following option

```
./tradee2e.sh -m down
```

This completes an end-to-end invocation of trade finance blockchain application from grounds up. Another approach of building the blockchain application could be through an open development framework called Hyperledger Composer. Hyperledger Composer is an extensive, open development toolset and framework that makes developing blockchain applications easier. You can use Hyperledger Composer to quickly model assets, business networks, and transactions methods. The Hyperledger Composer generates an archive file that can be deployed to the blockchain network. Hyperledger Composer is under active development, and we would revisit the tooling environment in a later edition. For more details, refer to - https://hyperledger.github.io/composer/

Summary

In this chapter, we provided a detailed insight on Hyperledger Fabric and its core components. We depicted different stages of design and implementation approach. We showed you how to define business networks, design a network topology and then deploying the application on the network. We also briefed about the trade finance smart contract and walked you through its business methods. And finally, we demonstrated end-to-end test of our trade finance application.

To conclude, blockchain will be the key driver in creating the business network based on trust and provenance. In future, we could see different communication styles or patterns and framework that will help realize the potential in blockchain as the technology of future.

Dear Readers, Thank you for Reading.

We hope you enjoyed reading the book, and the information provided would be a valuable resource in your blockchain journey.

We will constantly be updating the book with the latest information. For latest updates on the book, kindly visit - http://navveenbalani.com/index.php/articles/enterprise-blockchain-book/

As an author, we strive for comments and feedback to improve our book, and would greatly appreciate if you could leave your valuable feedback. Please share your review and feedback at http://amzn.to/2hKXr86

Thank you.

Made in the USA
Columbia, SC
30 September 2018